PR AISE FOR *SEARCH*

MW00479037

Ok amo sinaakia'tsis itsiiyisaakatoom sspomoohtsi, iksimsstaan,
ksa hkomm kii niipaitapiiyssin.
li'k skaitsowa'p sinaap.
Kii Annayii

Thi s book leads you along a humble path to a place that touches the
rea lm of the Vision Quest – where you can look into another world.
Jan e has a powerful mind and heart and her story brings us back to our
ph sical nature, which is made up of Mother Earth and the elements. It
cor nects you to the land and to the core of who we are, the place where
we are all one. Honestly and beautifully written.

—CONRAD LITTLE LEAF • PIITA PIIKAON/EAGLE BEING,

Piikani interpreter at Head-Smashed-In Buffalo Jump World Heritage Site

A j ourney of light and love into the far horizons of the spirit.

—WADE DAVIS, National Geographic explorer,

author, photographer, anthropologist

Se rching for Happy Valley is a special travelogue that chronicles Jane
M rshall's quest for the inner and outer boundaries of the sacred. She
de scribes her time with Indigenous People in Morocco and Alberta, but
es ecially her heart is opened in the remote area of Tsum on the border
of Nepal and Tibet. Here she undertakes an intrepid pilgrimage to a holy
m ountain rarely seen by outsiders. This is a poetic and heartfelt account
of a search for innermost meaning reflected in an environment of vast
gr ndeur beyond the senses.

—JETSUNMA TENZIN PALMO, international Buddhist teacher,

founder of Dongyu Gatsal Ling Nunnery

Searching for Happy Valley: A Modern Quest for Shangri-La is for the inner pilgrim in all of us. Intrepid and sure-footed, Jane Marshall offers a modern lens into the ancient tradition of hidden valleys that exist around the world, from Morocco, to Alberta, Canada, to the Himalayas. These remote regions offer a place of physical refuge and spiritual sanctuary. Along the way, the author brings alive the travellers she meets, and the friends she makes, from First Nations Elders to the delightful Nepalese Tibetan nun, Ani Pema.

In luminous, tender writing, Marshall invites us to step out of our comfort zone and into our courage zone. To let the land imprint itself on us, rather than for us to leave even our footprints. At this time of climate devastation, her words create a sanctuary. An urgent reminder of all that we must protect before it's too late. By the end, you'll have dusted off your walking boots to discover the remote, wild regions near you. Written in gold-washed prose with clear-eyed wisdom, this is a travel memoir filled with light, love, and longing.

—**DR. CLAIRE SCOBIE**, author of *Last Seen in Lhasa:*
The Story of an Extraordinary Friendship in Modern Tibet

Jane Marshall's book transcends cultural boundaries in its charting of the geography of happiness, and it reveals that it's as much about what we bring to the places that inspire us as about what such places may reveal about human flourishing. *Searching for Happy Valley* is a timeless journey that shows us how wild and dangerous places are also the most intimate when, as Jane Marshall writes, "we touch them with love."

—**IAN BAKER**, author of *The Heart of the World: A Journey to Tibet's Lost Paradise*

I have seen what occurs when culture, spirituality, music and the earth are desecrated. Jane Marshall's writing conveys the importance of happy valleys and Tibetan Buddhist *beyul*. They are sacred places that protect Indigenous wisdom – places where we find healing and return to what is most important.

—**NGAWANG CHOEPHEL**, musician and filmmaker, *Tibet in Song*

Searching *for* Happy Valley

Searching *for* Happy Valley

A MODERN QUEST FOR SHANGRI-LA

Jane Marshall

Sonam Chödon· litsspahpowaawahkaa

RMB

For information on purchasing bulk quantities of this book, or to obtain media excerpts or invite the author to speak at an event, please visit rmbooks.com and select the "Contact" tab.

RMB | Rocky Mountain Books Ltd.
rmbooks.com
@rmbooks
facebook.com/rmbooks

Cataloguing data available from Library and Archives Canada
ISBN 9781771605731 (softcover)
ISBN 9781771605748 (electronic)

All photographs are by Jane Marshall unless otherwise noted.

Design: Lara Minja, Lime Design
Cover photo: Denis Belitsky/Shutterstock

Printed and bound in Canada

We acknowledge the financial support of the Government of Canada through the Canada Book Fund and the Canada Council for the Arts, and of the province of British Columbia through the British Columbia Arts Council and the Book Publishing Tax Credit.

Disclaimer
The views expressed in this book are those of the author and do not necessarily reflect those of the publishing company, its staff, or its affiliates.

FOR THE INDIGENOUS COMMUNITIES
OF THE HAPPY VALLEYS.

We would like to also take this opportunity to acknowledge the traditional territories upon which we live and work. In Calgary, Alberta, we acknowledge the Niitsítapi (Blackfoot) and the people of the Treaty 7 region in Southern Alberta, which includes the Siksika, the Piikuni, the Kainai, the Tsuut'ina, and the Stoney Nakoda First Nations, including Chiniki, Bearpaẃ, and Wesley First Nations. The City of Calgary is also home to Métis Nation of Alberta, Region III. In Victoria, British Columbia, we acknowledge the traditional territories of the Lkwungen (Esquimalt and Songhees), Malahat, Pacheedaht, Scia'new, T'Sou-ke, and W̱SÁNEĆ (Pauquachin, Tsartlip, Tsawout, Tseycum) peoples.

It seems to me...that these cultures hold a secret
to parts of us that have been lost in the West:
our ability to live in accord with nature and with spirit.

—**SHARON BLACKIE,** *If Women Rose Rooted*

CONTENTS

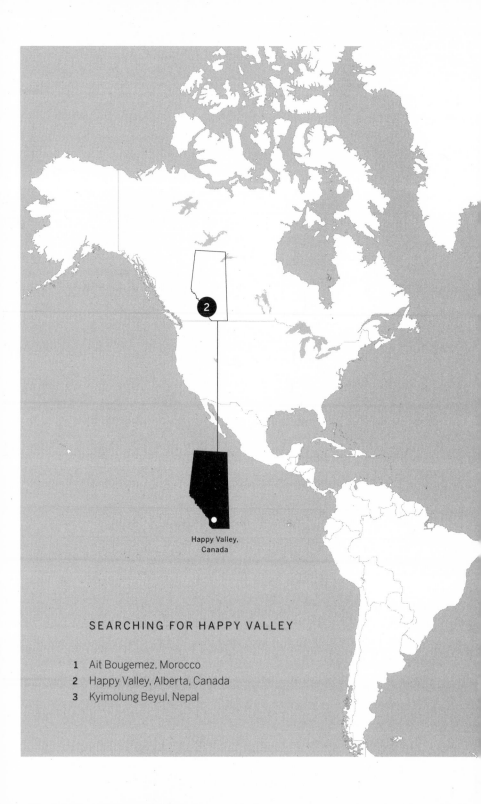

Happy Valley,
Canada

SEARCHING FOR HAPPY VALLEY

1 Ait Bougemez, Morocco
2 Happy Valley, Alberta, Canada
3 Kyimolung Beyul, Nepal

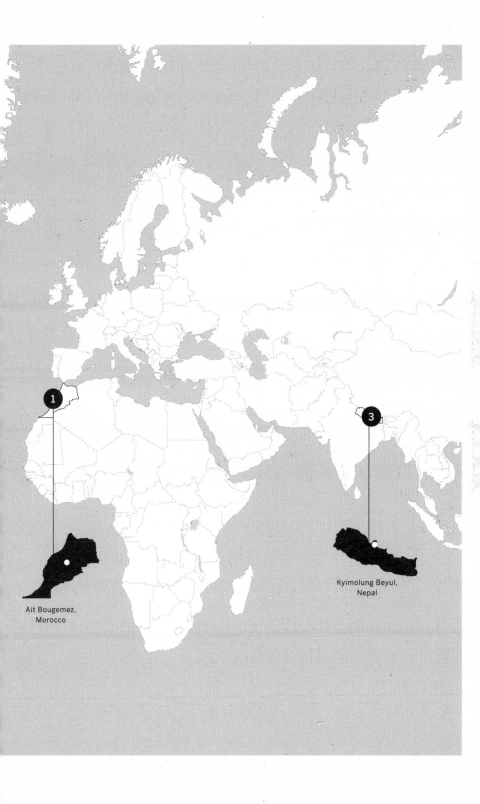

1

3

Ait Bougemez,
Morocco

Kyimolung Beyul,
Nepal

ACKNOWLEDGEMENTS

This book is a result of deep longing for our world's sacred places. I wish to first acknowledge the Indigenous Peoples who serve as caretakers for the happy valleys I've written about. Their wisdom and multigenerational experience are a model we can all learn from – cross-culturally, societally, globally and personally. It was extremely important to me to vet this book with members of the Indigenous groups I wrote about. Unintentional cultural bias is a tricky thing to navigate because it is often subconscious. I have done my utmost through research, collaboration, personal conversations and interviews to uncover and correct bias, mistakes and errors. Any remaining errors are fully my own based on my understanding at the time of writing this book. I did my best, from the bottom of my heart and with huge help.

That help came from the following people: Ahmad El-Allaly of the Amazigh people in Morocco read drafts of this book and shared anthropomorphic locations and Tamazight place names for the land in Happy Valley where he was raised. It is right that we use these names, since they are the original ones. Ahmad, thank you for guiding us into your ancestral land. Head-Smashed-In Buffalo Jump/Pissk'ān interpreter, Conrad Little Leaf/Piita Piikoan/Eagle Being of the Piikani people, read the Alberta section multiple times. He offered feedback and insight into his experience in residential schools, shared Niitsítapi history, and used his linguistics background to provide Sokitapi/Blackfoot names for people and places. We became close through our work together, and he bestowed upon me the name Iitsspahpowaawahkaa, which means "Walking Above." Conrad, your words gave me strength, and I will forever think of you as a Blackfoot Dalai Lama because of your warm heart. You gave me a name and pushed me off into the world. Head interpreter at Head-Smashed-In Buffalo Jump/Pissk'ān, Stanley Knowlton/ Rabbit in Motion of the Piikani people, read drafts and shared key information about Naapi and sacred places in Happy Valley, Alberta. Stanley, thank you for revealing to me the location of Naapi's heart, and for showing us all the connection between geography and spirit. The Owl Talks of the Kainai people read the manuscript and gave his blessing for me to write about the Sundance Ceremony, and welcomed my family into Ceremony on the reservation for a Sweat Lodge Ceremony. The Owl Talks, my family is grateful you showed us, in a first-hand way, the essence of Happy Valley. Morris Little Wolf, your stories soothe, and they bring us back to what's important. Despite great odds, you keep the teachings alive. We were honoured to come to your home and sweat with you.

Grandma, I'm so glad we got to explore Happy Valley together. I was tired out after our daily explorations long before you were! To Amy Paran, for being my friend and hiking partner, and for introducing me to Ken Williams. Ken, you have been my cultural connector with the Soki-tapi. Our conversations on Naapi's spine will forever inspire me. Thanks to Colton Red Young Man and Travis North Peigan (deceased) for collecting offerings for me to deposit in Nepal. To Sarah Strel, for sharing Betty Bastien's book, which provided a female Blackfoot perspective. To Bob Blaxley, author of *The Whaleback: A Walking Guide*, who took time for phone interviews and read an early draft. Thanks to the Alberta Wilderness Association for connecting me to Bob Blaxley and botanist Cheryl Bradley. Tony and Deb Webster, Grandma and I so enjoyed sitting with you and sharing stories.

The Nepal section of my book grew over many years and multiple Nepal trips. Tenzing Lhundup, a former abbot and Tsumpa monk from the Nile Labrang, and an expert on Kyimolung texts, vetted the book and helped with fact checking and accuracy. His uncle,

Lama Sherap Tendar Rinpoche, spiritual head of the Nile Labrang in Tsum, encouraged me to write about Kyimolung in English so more people could learn its history and power. I'm grateful I was able to follow the place guide the Nile Labrang has safeguarded. Dungse Lama Pema of the Tsum people, abbot of Thrangu Monastery Canada, and descendent of the great tertön Chokyi Wangchuk, shared valuable information on Kyimolung and his family lineage. Lama Pasang, former ward Chief of Lamagaun, Tsum and spiritual head of the Ngak Labrang, brother to Dungse Lama Pema and Dhawa Tashi, was truly supportive during my trips. We continue to work closely through the Compassion Project, a charity I co-founded with a key group of Tsum people, in Nepal. Dhawa Tashi, Compassion Project treasurer and brother of Dungse Lama Pema and Lama Pasang, helped secure me a spot on a helicopter, which gave me the gift of extra time in Tsum. Karma Rinpoche of Nubri Monastery (Serang) explained the significance of the main monastery temple at the foot of Tashi Palsang, and Khenpo David Karma Choephel kindly translated for me. Tanzin Gyaltsen Lama, mountain guide and Compassion Health Centre operations coordinator of the Tsum people of Nepal, wrote about his harrowing ordeal during our expedition in Nepal's Happy Valley when he was caught overnight on the mountain, and he read drafts and helped me fact check. His mountain skills made my dream to see Tashi Palsang real. What an adventure we had! I will be forever happy that I was able to travel to the heart of Kyimolung with Tibetan Buddhist nun Ani Pema of Drephuet Dronme Nunnery in upper Tsum. She was my Tsumpa sister, and she will always be alive in my heart despite her passing in 2022. Her strength, beauty, and courage inspired me and I often wonder how we were connected in our past lives. To Sangay Phuntsok for drawing two maps: one of Sarphu and one of Kyimolung beyul.

Yeshe Palmo was the secret key in all this. Without her courage in travelling to Tsum before it was open to tourists, and her subsequent thesis, map and commissioned translation, we would not have the richness of information we do today, or the foundation from which to keep exploring. Yeshe is strong, clear-minded and one of the most honest people I know. Thank you, my dharma sister. Renee Ford sent me a book about Shambhala and impressed on me that I really *must* meet her friend, Yeshe Palmo. Eric Fabry's beyul research helped with my own and made it more complete. Neil Haggard, my adventure travel book friend, edited a draft and gave helpful feedback, and so did my mom, Jan Marshall. Claire Scobie, author of *Last Seen in Lhasa*, was generous of heart to read my manuscript, provide an endorsement and edits, and to share her own beyul adventures with the world. Thank you to Drakar Rinpoche for our friendship, karmic connection, and for giving me my Tibetan name, Sonam Chödon. I hope to find you in all my future lives.

I'd like to acknowledge the Alberta Foundation for the Arts for awarding me a project grant. It's extremely hard for artists to have time and funds to dive fully into their craft, and the grant made a huge difference. Thanks to Roth and Ramberg Photography for the breathtaking photo of Conrad Little Leaf on his people's sacred ground.

To my husband, Mike, and children, Ben and Julie: Thank you for understanding my need for travel, and for being part of this story. Now it's time for all of us to thrive in our own Happy Valley in Canmore.

All the effort and love for this project have helped me create the most true pathways into the happy valleys, so readers can come on this epic journey too.

Note: For Tibetan and Nepali place names, I used the most commonly recognized spellings. These can vary widely on maps and in guidebooks.

INTRODUCTION

The voice of my grandfather travels through the folds of my mind:
It's so peaceful
In the valley...
He'd sing this verse of an unknown song on trails perfumed with wild Alberta sage, where husky prairie grass met the roll of the Rocky Mountains. He was a quiet man with a blue inner longing. But in the peaceful valleys just west of his home in the ranch town of High River, Alberta, he'd brighten. The sun would soak into his ironed plaid shirt, would warm his tobacco-stained hands. He chain-smoked Winston cigarettes and drank black coffee from a Thermos, always sweetened with farm honey. My grandpa died in 2001, but his spirit still speaks to our family, especially in the quiet in-between times.

When I was 14, Grandpa taught me to drive on rural gravel roads that pointed toward those valleys, in a space between domestic and wild. I'd sit at the wheel of his tan Oldsmobile station wagon. Scotch mints in the console. Stale scent of upholstery laced with the smoke of a thousand cigarettes. In the company of a man who did not abuse silence.

Tires crunched gravel.

The open road took us in, and for a few hours we'd become nameless.

Wordless.

Free.

Grandpa's longing must have pressed into my mind. As a young woman, I'd make solo pilgrimages from my home in Edmonton to the province's wild places, finding my own way back to nature.

Once, I borrowed my mom's Pontiac 6000 to venture beyond my driving training grounds into Kananaskis Country. Through autumn gold poplars, I walked alone to the base of a gleaming waterfall. In my pocket was one of my baby teeth. My mom had saved them from my childhood, and once I learned the tooth fairy wasn't real, she returned them to me. I felt its glossy calcium formations between the pads of my finger and thumb. It could have been a tiny white shell. Or a stone. I felt the intense need to do more than just look at the scene before me. I wanted to become it. And so I threw my little tooth in. A shard of Jane in the waterfall.

I'd do this at special locations with my other teeth, or I'd pull out a lock of hair and bury it in the dirt. Maybe I was strange, but I later learned that Tibetan pilgrims wandering to sacred places leave pieces of their clothing, hair or teeth. And a wise Piikani First Nations man from southern Alberta I interviewed for a Travel Alberta article, Conrad Little Leaf/Piita Piikoan/Eagle Being, told me that it's tradition to offer water or food to the earth at sacred sites. These impulses are a form of giving and connection. Instead of tromping the earth and taking photos, plucking her wildflowers and stealing her stones, hunting her animals for wall trophies, mining and extracting her treasures, carving her into range roads and townships, slicing her skin with road-building machinery, plotting her, mapping her, using her, eating her and spitting her out, instead, we give. And in the soft act of giving, that's when we receive.

I've been searching for Happy Valley my whole life. Perhaps my grandpa's wandering ways imprinted on me too deeply, like footprints on rain-soaked mud, forming a path I had to follow. Perhaps that was his plan all along.

This search for Happy Valley isn't mine alone. It's the age-old quest for Shangri-La, coded into the very dips and valleys of our human DNA.

As a travel writer, I've visited places across our planet, and I've noticed a theme. In seemingly unrelated cultures, there exist sacred valleys where a balance between humans and nature has been struck. These places are considered sacred geography by their Indigenous Peoples, and they share key characteristics: they are remote and geographically protected by mountains; they are home to rare plants and animals; they exist outside of protection zones, which gives them autonomy but makes them vulnerable; and they are places where inhabitants have lived with advanced subsistence technologies for millennia. And, importantly, in Shangri-La women are honoured as a balancing, powerful force.

Local people know each of these valleys as "Happy Valley," and I became hungry to know just what made them so. I found the first Happy Valley writing my first book, *Back Over the Mountains*. It is called Kyimolung in ancient texts and is located in the high Himalayas of Nepal. There are no roads to get there, and it takes days of intense hiking to access it. Its inhabitants are Tibetan Buddhists, and the valley holds eighth-century treasures and texts hidden within mountains, monasteries and caves. Two years later, I found another Happy Valley by following red-crystal dust trails into the Atlas Mountains of Morocco with my husband and our two children. There we immersed ourselves in Amazigh/Berber culture by doing village homestays and travelling to a goat-herding hut where Muslim families live off the land and animals. Then my grandmother surprised me by telling me there's a Happy Valley right in our province of Alberta, and that it was there where we had spread my grandfather's ashes.

The question is, why should we care about these happy valleys? What makes them significant? In truth, our human future depends on them. In Tibetan Buddhism, Shangri-La is believed to be a place of refuge where people can survive in times of strife, war and environmental devastation. An ideal place where people live in harmony with the environment. For me, happy valleys have been a place to reconnect with nature and reset myself when life gets too neurotic. The scientific community has proven that our planet is heating up, our ocean reef systems are collapsing, and life as we're living it is unsustainable. We are also facing times of unprecedented anxiety and polarization. Renowned anthropologist and past National Geographic Society explorer in residence Wade Davis asserts that it is time to look to the ancient wisdom of cultures that lived on this earth with incredible primal technologies for thousands of years before industrialization. That now, before it's too late, we must learn from our elder brothers and sisters. Unfortunately, dominant colonial governments have destroyed much of this knowledge over a remarkably short time period – a few hundred years or so in Canada, currently in Tibet, and with a potential threat of spreading to Nepal, and in the 20th century with French colonization in Morocco – laying waste to languages, rituals, entire animal species and what were deemed to be "barbaric Native ways."

The time to find Shangri-La is now. We need to see and feel the deep peace that still exists hidden in these happy valleys and within their keepers, and to recognize the ill effects when happy valleys are exploited and subjugated. By searching for Happy Valley, we have the opportunity to learn – and to return.

1

Ait Bougemez, Morocco
January 2014

The Bergerie

THE MULE'S HOOVES pick their course toward the crumbling Aguerd N'Almane, the Pass of Safety. It is a sag in Morocco's High Atlas Mountains that will lead us to the mountain hut. My children sway upon the animal's back and stare wide-eyed. The trail is a porous carpet of stone dust in shades of ochre, russet and rose. Twisted pines stretch skyward, beautifully pained and made arthritic by their life at 2140 m. Their bark splits like open sores. Geographical frontiers like this always get my heart racing. I've learned that, in places where naked stone overtakes the flora, where mountains heave and the sun shatters into prisms, there are junctures where the familiar world loses its grip.

Our guide Ahmad and his cousin Mohamed lead us over the col into the paradisiacal lands that cradle their family's mountain hut. "The Bergerie," our guide Ahmad calls it, illuminating Morocco's colonial French history, and he annunciates with a sense of wonder and pride. It is a remote, high-altitude hut where people live according to the life cycle of their goats and the changing of seasons, maintaining the semi-nomadic, pastoral lifestyle of their Amazigh/Berber ancestors. This magical mountain house is called Ahbak in Ahmad's Indigenous language, and so that is what I will call it in this book. As with so many Indigenous cultures, the original people of this land had their places renamed by outside forces. The word "Berber" that much of the world is familiar with is akin to "foreigner" or "barbarian." Understandably, the mountain people of the Atlas prefer to be called Amazigh. It means "Free People."

My heart trips as we crest the pass and descend to Ahbak. It is all I'd hoped for. It's the place I always search for, have searched for in Tibet, Nepal, the Canadian Rockies, and am now finding in North Africa in yet another form. I take a moment to divert off the path and lean against the trunk of a gargantuan juniper tree. The parched bark scratches my back as I gaze up through its intricate branch system. The crown blooms round and wide. A stream guides us on. It blinks weak winter light off its surface, then slides through dormant apple and almond orchards to make its way to the hut. En route we meet Ahmad's cousin Said, who is out for the day with his herd. Meeting Said is like touching a lightning bolt. His presence is crisp, the air around him charged with a piercing, all-seeing nature. His eyes are green meteors flashing with desert fire. He spends his days hiking with only a dagger in his belt and small satchel across his chest, combing the hills with his four-legged charges. His eyes see everything; they know the very texture of this land. Nature has eroded all pretense, and it's hard to tell the man from the mountains.

At dusk, Ben and Julie, ages 10 and 7, hop across the hills and help guide Said's bleating animals back to their pen. Ahmad and I watch from a hill above, and as I sit with him, I watch the tenor of the land seep into him. He confides that Said is the best man he knows. That, after too long in the city of Azilal, where he lives and runs his trekking business from, caught up in business matters and modern life, it's here that he yearns for. He spent his childhood days with Said wandering the High Atlas Mountains, and this connection with the land imprinted on Ahmad – like my grandpa's had on me.

"I love my cousin so much. This is my favourite place on Earth." The words float from Ahmad's mouth across the crumbling mountain layers to where Said expertly navigates the animals' nightly return. They will sleep in the home's inner courtyard, cradled in the safety of thick clay walls. While many other Amazigh nomads now flock to the cities in search of the promised modern life, Said remains. Maybe he knows something they don't.

"This life requires, how do you say..." Ahmad searches beyond the memory stores of his native language, Tamazight, then through the country's official Arabic, perhaps next through French, Morocco's second language and the mother tongue of many of his trekking clients, to dig deep for the most meaningful English word.

"Solidarity. In the city, there is the mentality of individualism. But in the mountains, it is of solidarity. The mountain life is hard but happy."

Everything in the valley is shared. Water, wood, the pastures and the work. Everyone respects the collective resources because the survival of the community depends on it. I'm honoured my family has been granted access to this Happy Valley, and to the tendrils of ancestry that extend from Ahmad deep into the earth and its history. Through Ahmad, we, too, belong to the land, even for just these few days.

Later, we sit for mint tea on the family's floor. There's no toilet (not even an outhouse), and no running water. Said's wife, Malika, cooks in an earthen-floor kitchen by way of the last remaining light that seeps through a lone window. She squats to knead dough for our daily bread.

I'd wanted Ben and Julie to witness a place where humans live simply, where the connection between earth, seed and stomach is clear. I'm always searching for such spots where a balance has been struck, where humans find a way to be at peace, not only with their immediate environment but also with themselves.

Just how did I find this Happy Valley? Finding Shangri-La usually requires a series of linked events, like in James Hilton's famous novel *Lost Horizon*, where a plane crashes in the Himalayas and delivers travellers to a mysterious and idyllic realm where people do not age. It's a circuitous path requiring effort, will, and often luck.

I'd been in Nepal in the Happy Valley of Tsum two years prior, a sacred valley deemed by locals to be one of several hidden

Shangri-Las in the Himalayas. Then, as my family and I began planning a trip to Morocco, I somehow learned of Ait Bougemez, also coined "Happy Valley." An African Happy Valley? I was shocked by the photos I saw on the internet; they looked remarkably like Nepal despite being separated by space and culture. We planned a one-week guided trip with Intrepid Travel to become acquainted with the country of Morocco. Then I allotted another week for Happy Valley, Ait Bougemez. Trouble was, I had no idea how we'd get there.

Morocco

WE STAND AS A FAMILY OF FOUR in the souks of Marrakesh. If we were the centre of the universe, this would be the cosmic organization: Us, squashed by Moroccan shoppers and vendors and mules dragging wooden carts. Whining motorcycles honk their horns, and in an act of African magic, they part the tides, which close in their wake like colourful curtains. All this is squeezed into shopping lanes by silver teapot stands and fabric stands, carpet stands and leather shoe stands. There are candy bar stands and lantern stands and custom leather belt stands. It's like gravity is crushing us with an inward pressing of life and small-scale economics. Further out in orbit are the artisans who supply the vendors; multigenerational tanneries and metal bashers, and leather cutters and yarn-dyeing vats tinted red, gold and blue. All this is held together by 19 kilometres of long, adobe-style walls as dense as two metres, built back in the 12th century. Outside these walls, a modern city of almost one million vibrates with life. The Atlantic Ocean laps Morocco's western shores, and the Atlas Mountains punctuate the desert sky to the east. Beyond that: the shifting sands of the Sahara.

We're berthed into Marrakesh's Djemaa El Fna square, where cobras dance for their charmers and collared monkeys do tricks for their cloaked handlers. The kids are overwhelmed. Mike and I are overwhelmed. The sun sets and, as it does, the square reaches a fever pitch. It's a fantastical sensory display, but we want out. Mohammed, our curly-haired Amazigh guide, leads us from the square to a rooftop restaurant named after his tribal home in the Atlas Mountains. Ait Bougemez. It's our last night with him, and we dine on couscous and roasted root vegetables that shine with olive oil in the clay tagine. Mohammed makes final plans for us to meet up with his friend Ahmad, a mountain guide in Happy Valley.

I found our connection to this African Shangri-La a few days earlier in the seaside town of Agadir. We'd been eating scrambled eggs in a blue and white restaurant when Mohammed joined our family at a wobbly metal table. I'd known about Happy Valley from research at home, and just needed to figure out how to get there, so I asked Mohammed. Maybe he knew how?

"You want to go there? I'm so surprised!" he'd said, his mass of curls even tighter in the ocean's off-spray. "That is where I am from. Not many tourists know about my valley. I know one friend I can trust. He can help you." So we solidified a trip to the spine of mountains separating the Sahara Desert from the Atlantic Ocean.

Journey into Ait Bougemez

JULIE, BEN, MIKE AND I meet our new guide, Ahmad, in the desert town of Azilal, the capital of the central High Atlas. It will be our staging point. Ahmad is instantly likeable. He has a goatee and moustache and thick black hair. He's burly like Mike, and his eyes are soft but keen, watching everything, taking stock of us, making sure we're comfortable and offering gentle lifts to the corners of his mouth as we make our way through pink, multi-story, desert city houses. He speaks mostly to the kids. Makes this fun. We head to his house, where he lives with his wife, Keltouma, daughter, Rihab, and relatives. It's home base, and his family chose to settle there so they could remain close to Happy Valley but still have access to modern amenities. Ahmad guides mostly French trekkers and he's often gone for weeks, which suits his ancestral imprints for nomadic life. The Amazighs were/are tribal, moving with the flow of weather in the high North African landscape. They are a distinct cultural group and speak a different language from the majority of Arabic-speaking Moroccans.[1]

We must trust Ahmad to lead us into Happy Valley. He's our link.

We begin with a meal in his home before setting off for the valley. There are several visiting family members who have just arrived from Ait Bougemez to do some shopping here in the city. They trickle into the eating room, and we sit together on benches pressed up against the walls. Keltouma emerges, hijab over her hair. A big tagine with goat meat is placed on the table, and when Ahmad explains that I'm a vegetarian, one of the women gasps, then covers her mouth with a hand. To survive in the mountain villages without meat seems unthinkable to her. Goat herding, meat eating, is woven into her culture.

Ahmad's daughter kisses my cheek as we prepare to depart, then we hop in an old Mercedes taxi and the bulls-eye symbol points us toward the mountains.

The peaks rear up, their snow glossy with old sun crust. The road draws us toward them along the most circuitous path. Where are we going? What will it be like? Our eyes pop at the scenery, at the unknown, except for Julie's. My little girl has fallen asleep beside me in the back seat. But not for long. Julie wakes up

---

1   The Amazigh people speak three dialects: Tarifit, Tamazight and Tachelhit.

just enough to vomit across the vinyl – and all over her clothes. The mountain road is too much for her stomach.

The taxi driver pulls over as if this is completely normal. I bet he's glad he has vinyl seats. Village children run to see who we are, and Ahmad shields Julie, back turned, so I can get her changed. A gutter holds a downhill flow of water and I rinse out her shirt in the grit. As a mom, I've never been great at being prepared with Kleenex or Band-Aids, etc., but this time I'm all over it. I have wet wipes in my travel bag, and I clean the taxi seat until it shines, all while wondering is this going to be too much for the kids? Because I'm aiming for total immersion. I've asked Ahmad if we can sleep in village homes as I had done in Nepal. I know Happy Valley can't be accessed through typical travel, or by implanting our own ideas of comfort and "the way things should be" onto reality. Such valleys ask us to let go of our regular ways of thinking, our habits, our attitudes, and sometimes our basic comforts. But am I asking too much of our elementary-aged kids? I'm desperate for them to see beyond the scope of Western life, not because our way is bad, but because it's just *one way*. I want them to know what it's like to rely on the land for shelter and food. I want them to become children of the world.

The taxi whines as we snake higher, higher. Our adrenaline climbs too.

We finally arrive at Ahmad's in-laws' family guest house. It protrudes from the hillside above, a note in a symphony of other buildings layered up the valley wall. We activate our legs on the large number of stairs that ascend to the front entrance. This guest house, called a *gîte* in French, was built about 80 years ago during their grandparents' time as their family home. Now it has been transformed into a place where people like us are invited to stay.

In the main gathering room, Ahmad changes. He swaps his city clothes for a *jellaba*, and, in doing so, he slides into another world completely. It's the traditional garb of the mountain people and looks just like what Obi-Wan Kenobi wore in *Star Wars*. Ahmad's goal as a trekking guide is to introduce guests to his land and its people through their linguistic richness, clothing, traditional songs, cooking, and all that characterizes them. We play charades near the fireplace and try to keep our feet warm on the rich, thick rugs. The night smothers us in darkness, holding us in a cold embrace.

I'm not the only one who has noticed the Happy Valley similarities between Nepal and Morocco. Some travel guides say Ait Bougemez feels like a hidden Himalayan kingdom dropped into the Atlas. Having been in both, I strongly agree.

Its origin story is that, one million years ago, the valley was a natural dam. The land collapsed and gave birth to a fertile area where cereals, vegetables and trees can be cultivated between 1700 and 2300 metres in elevation.

Until the year 2000, the only access to Ait Bougemez was by old gravel road, or by foot over a 2800-metre-high pass. Ahmad's father and other villagers would make the two-day walk over the high pass to Rose Valley to sell oil and to buy dates and henna. Now a paved (if narrow) road has been pulled across the hills at the valley's opposite entrance, making it possible to drive from Azilal. Until recently, it was cut off from the world for four months of the year due to snow, and there are no marked trekking routes, so finding your way along the network of old caravan trails and donkey paths requires the services of an experienced guide. I'm happy we're with Ahmad. The road has brought the benefit of schools, and now girls and adults, who never learned to read or write as children, are receiving education. The valley is about 30 km long, with a few offshoots. There is a small health centre nearby that services the villages.

After a breakfast of flatbread, sweet mint tea, Laughing Cow cheese, and jam, Ahmad draws us from the cold clay walls out into the valley. The landscape is whitewashed, or rather, gold-washed, with sideways winter sunlight. The leafless trees cast long shadows. The valley floor is an expertly cultivated patchwork quilt of dormant nourishment: apple, almond, and gigantic walnut trees, and barley and root vegetable crops – especially potatoes and turnips. Alfalfa is grown for the animals. Between the gardens are short stone walls delineating the harvest of each family, and an intricate series of handmade irrigation canals hydrates the land, drawing water from the stream to each plot. Water is considered sacred, and therefore all the families participate in the maintenance of the irrigation canals. The village council is elected annually and ensures that this tradition of shared responsibility is respected for the good of the village, the greater community and the whole valley. Human need and nature have a pact here, and the land is used well. Loved well. It seems to know its farmers, and in return for the water and hand-reared care, it returns healthy harvests. Smoke rises from the pink-tan homes, then lingers just above the straw rooftops in a fairy-like haze.

We pass beyond the last homes of Ahmad's village and turn back to look. Now we can see the shape of the valley and the protective hills that rise up on each side. The village is a dome of terraced homes that wrap around a protruding part of the valley wall. The top has been left uninhabited in a seeming homage to the sky. The houses are made from the earth, which has been dug, pulled up, then re-formed into walls with a few windows for light. Here people use their mud-maize rooftops for working and enjoying the view, and drinking piping hot mint tea from glass cups. The abodes, so unlike most homes in Edmonton, are a reworking of nature rather than a separation from it.

"It's called Ikhf N'Ighir," says Ahmad. *Ikhf* means "head," he tells me, and *ighir* means "shoulder." I see what he means as we gaze at the village from the vantage point. The rise looks like a strong and rounded shoulder supporting the homes, and, above, the head gazes across the valley.

The Amazigh/Berbers see themselves in the context of the land. Ait Bougemez is an Indigenous word that means "those in the middle." Geographically, they are in the very centre of North

Africa's highest range, the High Atlas, hugged tight on all sides. According to Ahmad, the High Atlas Mountains are divided further into three parts. "Happy Valley," explains Ahmad, "is the middle of the very middle of the High Atlas." Without realizing it, we have come to the epicentre of this great range. He goes on to tell me that the village Ait Imi in Happy Valley translates as "mouth," "passage," or "door." It's located at an elevation of 2905 metres and provides "access between tribes." Ait is an Amazigh word that means "the children of," and so each village is like a mother, and its inhabitants, her kin.

Google Earth provides an interesting view. Natural life pools in the valley bottom in shades of green, hungering for water and human connection, while sepia-toned mountains rise on all sides like protective guardians. Indeed, we have found a hidden paradise where precious life is protected. The middle of the middle, the heart of the High Atlas.

Ahmad takes us to a UNESCO World Heritage Site called Siddi Moussa. We walk the level valley floor, then see a large pyramid of land rising from the valley's centre. It's in a seemingly unnatural location. I can't tell if it's naturally occurring or human made. A large circular building crowns the top. We climb.

A young man appears at the door, and we realize this building is being guarded. It has been for centuries, for this is where the villagers kept their grain stores and precious belongings. The main guardian is 105 years old,[2] but Ahmad says he can't always make the steep climb up, and so this substitute guardian sizes us up from his post, leaning his body against a rough-hewn timber doorframe. His hands are stuffed deep in both pockets. Sun smacks his face. He looks like a bouncer, and has the appropriate level of seriousness and judgment. One half of the double doors behind him is open, and an inky, mysterious blackness leaks out.

Essentially, this site is an earthen safe deposit box, like a local bank. It is composed of 30 small "rooms," traditionally used to

---

2 The guardian has now passed away.

keep all the families' precious goods – cereals, pulses, jewels and important documents – each with a unique wooden key. In the past, when there were conflicts, the granary also served as a refuge for women and children.

It's also a sacred place, and this is what interests me most. At the centre of this dark circle is the tomb of the saint, Siddi Moussa.

"He was a great healer," explains Ahmad as he lights two taper candles and hands them to Ben and Julie, who duck into a tiny inner sanctum. We follow, and huddle in the black, seeing what the candlelight will illuminate.

"Tsk tsk." The universal sound of disapproval comes from between Ahmad's teeth. The stones atop the grave have been disturbed, and the guardian tells us that robbers were searching for treasure. Ahmad feels the granary's architectural and spiritual heritage is being neglected, and I think of how much Indigenous history is lost simply by the world not paying attention, or preferring to place its attention on the histories of colonizers or the dominant political agenda.

This is a site still used by pilgrims, especially women who wish to conceive. On Thursdays, they make the climb and present a strip of material from their clothing as an offering before entering the tomb. Then they stay overnight in the womb-like enclosure and pray for fertility. The stone sucks up all sound; the stillness is profound.

On the hike home, we hear the muezzin's call to prayer vibrate through Happy Valley. This happens five times daily. In the city, Muslims go to the mosque to pray, but here in Happy Valley they simply put down their hoes, unroll their prayer rugs and bow to the earth, head pointed to Mecca. I'm struck by how people here are so connected to the land. The land is their mother. They do not harm her. They do not bleed her dry. I see a direct balance of giving and receiving. The villagers till the land until it can breathe, using mules and their own strong forearms. They draw water to the canals to quench her earthen thirst. They add nutrients from tubers, and they infuse her pores with sound from the mosques, then prostrate their bodies so their very human cells connect with the ground below.

Circling Back to Ahbak, January 4

Another hiking day. Lunchtime. We sit at a picnic spot at the edge of a farm plot at Ait Wanougdal village, where the valley has no choice but to give way to the rising hills. The poplar bark gleams silver, and the sky is painted potent blue. Ahmad has brought a simple meal of boiled potatoes (which we sprinkle salt on), tomatoes, handmade bread, olives, tinned mackerel, and dates and oranges for dessert.

Our walk to this spot has me struck with wonder. There is electricity in the homes, and there is education and accessible health care (though the Amazigh people had to fight for these rights) – yet people are living traditionally. They are connected to their ancestors through their very homes, which have been passed down for generations and modified with love and need with each new family. What would it be like to live this way all the time? To belong to the land? I think of how the majority of Canadians like me are descended from European immigrants, and how we lost our ancestral connections to the land. Ahmad's roots are obvious and deep. I wonder where my own are. Are they in my home city of Edmonton, Alberta? My family has lived there for less than 40 years. Are they in Calgary, where I was born? Perhaps in southern Alberta, where my grandma was raised as a farm girl on the prairies? There is a strange gap inside me, a gap that leaves me floating and untethered. I seek out these cultures and the places that grew them so I can see, name and understand this gap inside, and better understand my lack of belonging.

Butterflies dance among thick blades of grass as we munch on our food. Ahmad hears something in the grass, then spots a puppy. He coaxes it over with the promise of a treat. Julie has always loved dogs, even though she was once bitten quite badly by one.

She was more upset that the dog didn't like her than she was of the tooth marks it left on her eyebrow and chin. This little pup is young, with soft hair and slithery skin it still needs to grow into. Julie takes it into her arms and bathes it with love. Ahmad explains (out of earshot of Julie) that rabies is a problem here, and that each summer there's a campaign to shoot infected dogs. He looks at the pup and says that its mother is gone and that it won't survive. When it's time to move on, Julie refuses. She holds the dog, and in her young mind realizes for herself that it's not going to make it on its own. "How can we just *leave* it here?" she cries. I know Mike, Ben and I are thinking the exact same thing. Yet we extricate the puppy from her grasp. Julie sobs into her dad's chest, and he holds her until the internal earthquake has moved through.

Life and death are apparent in this Shangri-La. Though humans wish for utopia and long life in a "perfect" place, the truth is that life is naked and raw, and death is real and unhidden. Perhaps the tradeoff for such vivid, visceral landscapes and experiences is that death is included in it all. We are granted the entire picture, and we must become strong enough to endure it. On market day, we saw goat meat displayed in the open air, the severed heads in proud prominence to demonstrate freshness. One can even go to the slaughter area to see the entire process. For a Western mind, this may seem gruesome. Yet it is the truth for each animal whose body parts we see so neatly dissected, packed into Styrofoam and cling-wrapped at the grocery store. In Happy Valley, you get the whole story.

Let's circle back now to Ahbak, the mountain hut where this story began. Its geometric walls sit partway up a mountain. Behind, the only way is up. The front views float off the slope across the open landscape. Unlike the homes in the main valley, it has no electricity, running water or heat. The lack of an outhouse will result in

Julie refusing to "go" for over 24 hours. The designated area for bathroom breaks is a terrace ledge with a nest of cedar boughs. "No problem!" says Ahmad, encouragingly.

I head outside to a maize-encrusted terrace. I am beyond my own thoughts and lost in the sensations of this place. The smell is of farm animals and dust, dry in my nostrils. The late day sun bakes my skin. Sounds: a donkey braying and the flutter of wings as chickens scatter; the call of a boy's voice. The sky is flawless blue and domes the view. Huge old junipers curl up from the earth beyond the house, intermingling with cultivated walnut and almond trees without any sense of competition. A fly buzzes by. Ahmad knows every tree and every part of this land with the intimacy of a great love story.

In the evening, Julie and Ben find their way to the inner courtyard and play with the baby goats. Julie lifts one into her arms, and it melts into her loving embrace. The kids love the cows and animals and being outside all day.

Ahmad is in his element and enjoys seeing how much we love Ahbak.

He tells me about his grandmother.

"She is 105 now. In winter she must go to Marrakesh because of the cold. But she'll never be happy in the city." It was this way for my grandfather too. And now for me. When I've been in the city too long, a slow inner death occurs. The revival comes only from placing my body back in the land. Love brings both joy and longing.

We are given a room to sleep in. The four of us line up in a row, and Ahmad tucks us in beneath piles of blankets, while the floor sucks heat from our bodies without mercy. The night bathes us in unrelenting blackness. Mike is feeling unwell, and by morning he's much worse. He hasn't slept properly in days. His face is grey; even his lips are an ashen hue. A fever has started and he has a headache – a cymbals-clashing, drums-beating kind of headache. Whatever virus or bug has penetrated his system is reaching its crescendo. He pulls up his hood as if to protect his aching body.

The timing seems to play out an old storyline for Mike and me. I have an insatiable appetite for travel, and I prefer simple living. If I could trade my house for a van, or a life in a mountain cabin, I would. Done! I have a nomadic vein too, a primal urge to travel and know the multiple cultures, languages and realities of the big earth. When I was in university, I got a part-time job at an outdoor adventure store so I could take a year off and travel in Southeast Asia. Mike joined me for part of the journey and says he never would've done it without me. My wandering ways opened up a big experience for him. I am like the wind, the sky, and Mike loves this about me. Mike is like the earth. He anchors and steadies me. I love his strong body, his wide muscles, his big brown-green eyes and unquestionable loyalty to friends and family. He's the guy who is always there to help and support. Together, we work. Yet we both admit that sometimes each of us compromises too much for the other.

Mike's illness at Ahbak strikes a tender chord inside. I don't want to leave this high mountain place, but Mike needs comfort. I'm worried about my husband and hope he hasn't contracted something dangerous. We load our backpacks and put the kids on the mule, waving goodbye to Ahmad's extended family. Mike forges ahead, the lure of a warmer bed and lower elevation pulling him with unfathomable force. He is too weak to speak and is focused on one thing only: getting back to the guest house.

Mike makes a recovery, mostly by reclining his sick body in the front room where he can receive the most solar gain. His strength slowly returns. In the meantime, the kids have been exploring the hillside and making friends with the milking cow and her calf. Ben has been scaling the ridge behind the guest house like a wild goat. They are dusty and dirty and so alive. As Mike recovers, I watch him slowly sink into this place. I watch him get comfortable with the uncomfortable. I watch him grow and feel a deep well of love for his willingness to try.

When we begin our departure from Ait Bougemez, I spot something at the bottom of the guest house steps. It's the glint of a silver CD left without a case on the rock. I pick it up. It's Deva Premal, one of my favourite yoga singers. Her music is often the backdrop to the yoga classes I teach.

"It's so strange," I say to Ahmad and Mike, turning it over in my hands. It's hardly even scratched. "This is the music I used to make a short film about my trip to Nepal." I'm always alert to connections like this. I place it in my bag and gratefully receive the offering. Ahmad later tells me that there is a quotation he likes very much. It says, "There is no coincidence. There are meetings and appointments of life." Something is indeed meeting, weaving itself together inside of me. It is a narrative already written that I'm just learning to read. The story of happy valleys and what they have to teach us.

Back in Azilal, we spend the night with Ahmad, Keltouma and their daughter in their family home. It's like a decompression zone after the intensity of Happy Valley. Keltouma takes me to the village *hammam* (bath). The women there seem to tease me a little in their local language, and I soon find myself stripped down to my panties and feeling rather exposed. We enter a steamy room and proceed to spend an unfathomable amount of time washing. First, we use black soap and slowly rub it all over our bodies. Every woman here does the same cleaning ritual, and each is at a different point in the process. There are grandmothers, mothers, young women and kids too, who wince and whine as their moms scrub their skin pink. The props include plastic buckets, sponges, soaps and scrubbers. It feels a bit like a feminine cleaning picnic.

The black soap is slippery and must be left on for a time. Then it is rinsed off with buckets of water. Next comes vigorous scrubbing. We wear coarse gloves and scrub, scrub, until layers of skin begin to curl off. I never imagined my own skin would do this! It's fascinating. I do a long, thorough scrub and rinse. I'm like a snake shedding her old skin. But when I think I'm done, I'm shown to scrub more.

Keltouma scrubs my back for me, and I surrender like a child. She lifts my left arm to get under my triceps, works down to my hip, then finds my back and rubs down the sides of my spine. I haven't been this well scrubbed since it was my own mother's hands doing the job.

We don't stop until the gloves yield nothing but squeaky cleanness, then we pour buckets of water over ourselves in an act of purification. After, Keltouma wraps my head in a hijab. When I look at myself in the mirror, I see that black cloth has concealed my hair. My eyes are now the main physical focus of my appearance, and they shine blue and big as I take in my new look.

Mike also goes through the hammam on the men's side, and I wonder what he might be shedding.

As the sun sets, we walk through the maze of houses to the local market, and Mike disappears for a while. He's been sporting a thick beard this trip, and his hair has gotten long. He looks insanely gorgeous. When I begin to worry if the market has swallowed him, I spot him. At least, I think it's him. He has undergone his own purification process. His hair is neatly cut, and his skin is smooth from the barber's straight blade.

When we leave Morocco, we leave with clean eyes and bodies, and new ways of seeing. Ben and Julie leave with rural life embedded into their growing minds.

2

Southern Alberta, Canada
July 2017–December 2018

Discovery

It is a land where climate and soil conspired to create ideal conditions
for a sea of grass where bison and other animals thrived and where
the earliest inhabitants took nomadic possession, touched the land
lightly, and left behind only modest signs of their passage.

—**LIZ BRYAN**, *Stone by Stone: Exploring Ancient Sites on the Canadian Plains*

MY JOURNEY to Happy Valley in Alberta begins with my grandma,
Joyce Marshall, when she's 87 years old. She grew up on 16,000
acres of ranchland in southern Alberta. On the great flat prairies
she spent her childhood days milking cows and tending hens. She
loved the feeling of the birds' brown feathers when she reached
beneath their warm bodies for eggs. Grandma grew up being connected to the entire life cycle of her food. She knew the seasons
and the vegetables her family could produce, watched animals
being born, growing and then taken for meat, and even today she's
always looking at the sky and predicting the weather. You'll often
hear my grandma say, "Look! A chinook arch!" as she spots the
line in the sky that forms when warm ocean winds ride over the
mountains and collide with prairie cloud.

Her family reared and sold cattle. Excess meat was shared with
neighbours, or canned and kept in a root cellar, held at a stable
temperature in an underground embrace. Nothing was wasted.
She loved eating the chewy fibres of preserved beef, made soft
from storage in glass jars in the dark. Grandma knew a connection to her food and the earth that I've always respected.

I grew up in Edmonton in a "regular" neighbourhood. Our land was like the land of people living in cities: a house upon a lot, lovingly planted trees and a fence around a prescribed linear rectangle. I remember leaning against a mayday tree in that yard, hungering for wilderness, trying to dive myself deep into the soil to a place unmanipulated by human organization.

Grandma has many stories to share with me now, and my ears are hungry. They long for the vibrations that will connect me to ancestry and land.

As a girl, Grandma loved hiking with her schoolmates. But one area was off limits. Her parents told her never to walk across the Bassano dam onto Siksika First Nations land – the second-largest reserve in Canada. "And boy, did we listen," she says. "We were good kids, and it was treated as sacred ground."

Beyond, said her parents, were "Indian" burial grounds. The dead were wrapped in light cloth and hoisted onto platforms high in the tree canopy. Beloved possessions were placed around them, along with food and water. Over time, the elements eroded flesh and wood, and items sifted through the trees. "We were told to never touch the relics," says Grandma.

I imagine disobeying the great-grandparents I never met and ducking from the blazing sun and yellow smell of wheat, the endless flatness of a land early explorers suggested should never be farmed because it was just too damned difficult, into those forbidden grounds. I would tilt my head to seek out the tree cemetery. Then I'd pour my gaze over the earth, looking for bleached skulls and arrowheads. I would look, but I would never touch.

Grandma now lives in Edmonton, about a five-minute walk from my house. I was telling her about my search for happy valleys in Nepal and Morocco – such far-off places. "But Jane!" she exclaimed. "We have a Happy Valley right here in Alberta!" She tells me that my grandpa trailed horses through it as a young man, from his home in Calgary south to the Buckhorn Ranch before Highway 22 was constructed through its centre. It is a place he loved very much, and even tried to move to when his family was young – though his wish did not materialize. At age 71, Grandpa died of cancer and willed us to spread his ashes there, near the Oldman River, a river bearing the First Nations name Náápi-iítahtaa, the lifeblood of Happy Valley and the dry farms beyond. I remember ash spilling to the soil as I helped my family return his body to his most beloved spot: a stand of glacial erratics. I'd been searching for Happy Valley on the other side of the earth; Grandpa found his near home.

Oh the stars are the candles and they light up the mountains,
Mountains, altars of God.
Oh the place where I worship is the wide open spaces,
Where the sun warms the peaceful sod.

This hymn was recited at his Irish-style wake. I also wrote him this poem:

We'll feel you in the sun-drenched foothills, the smell of
    wild sage, and the wind that courses through the valley.
Your strong spirit will live forever in the beauty of your
    mountains.
We know where you are, Grandpa.

I knew he loved the land, but I never knew the deeper significance it had for him. There are stories for me to hear. There is work for me to do. Seventeen years after his death, I see his story weaving into my own. And so I ask Grandma: "Want to go on a road trip?"

This year marks Canada's 150th birthday, but I'm yearning to touch a history extending back much further. Happy Valley's limber pines that have formed in relentless wind for hundreds of years; over 10,000 years of Indigenous history; the mountains of the Kananaskis, 200 million years in the making, embedded with pink seashells and shark teeth. I'm ready to explore a wisdom culture right in my own backyard, as well as the stories of my own ancestors.

Before Grandma and I embark, I educate myself about the environment and landscape we'll be visiting. I've been trained to do this from years of travel writing for newspapers and magazines, as well as my first book. Travel writing has given me the gift of studying a place deeply – first through research, and then by full and intensely real immersion.

I start with Google Maps for a satellite perspective of Happy Valley. My fingers direct the view based on Grandma's local knowledge. I find the Livingstone Range, an insanely straight north-south wall that forms a protective western flank. The undulating Porcupine Hills, known in Blackfoot language as Kai'skááhp-soy'is,[1] are to the east, and a flat, wide valley bottom splays out in between. Just west of Happy Valley, and parallel to the Livingstone Range, the Continental Divide rises up. It's the highest part of our country. This geographic spine pokes up from the land, connecting cultures and environments from icy Alaska to the tip of South America. Its primordial glaciers feed rivers that flow to the Pacific, Arctic and Atlantic oceans.

Next I discover an organization called the Alberta Wilderness Association (AWA), the oldest wilderness conservation group in Alberta. It does environmental protection work in a region called the Livingstone-Porcupine, roughly corresponding with the area my grandma traditionally knows as Happy Valley. The AWA calls it one of the most diverse and iconic regions of Alberta. It has five distinct vegetation types: grassland, parkland, montane, subalpine and alpine. It's a place where bison once numbered in the tens of millions, where thousands of elk still migrate for winter because of its idyllic temperatures and chinook winds, where rare plants grow, and rough fescue grasslands soak up similar amounts

---

1   The Porcupine Hills are more accurately translated as the Porcupine Tail Hills, Kai'skááhp-soy'is.

of carbon dioxide per acre as tropical rainforests.[2] Here, in a geological embrace, is Alberta's Shangri-La.

Despite its inherent richness, the AWA says this area is under threat. Its prized resources – oil, timber and minerals – are being milked for industrial interests. The AWA calls their piecemeal harvesting approach "death by a thousand cuts."[3] Several years after my trip with Grandma, the Alberta government begins to sell leases to mining companies that aim to shear the heads off the mountains of this region for coal. These mines will contaminate precious headwaters, including the Oldman River itself, and put at risk millions of people's health, not to mention desecrate animals' natural habitat and the sacred ground of the area's Niitsítapi (First Nations).

The AWA connects me to an author named Bob Blaxley for more information. Bob wrote "A Walking Guide for the Whaleback Area: Moving through a Sacred Space" when working on his master's degree at the University of Calgary. His feet put on countless miles walking Happy Valley.

"That whole countryside is very special," says Bob when I ring him at his home in Calgary. "And it has been for a long time. Much longer than this society's been here. It was the best bison ground on the continent because the native grasses keep their nutritional value in winter."

---

2   The book *Ranching in "God's Country": The Waldron Grazing Co-Op*, by Doug Nelson (High River, AB: Redgra Productions Limited, 2013), states that rough fescue rangeland soaks up more CO_2 per acre than the Amazon rainforest, while my fact check with the AWA and botanist Cheryl Bradley, who has worked in rough fescue grasslands, explains that these grasslands store approximately 200 tonnes of carbon per hectare versus 250 tonnes of carbon per hectare in rainforests (similar amounts). The challenge, she says, is to preserve the grasslands so they can keep the sequestered carbon held within them.

3   Alberta Wilderness Association, "Livingstone-Porcupine," https://albertawilderness.ca/issues/wildlands/areas-of-concern/livingstone-porcupine/.

He tells me of the special plants in Happy Valley. "There's prairie parsley (*Lomatium dissectum*), with its finely dissected leaves. The roots can be made into a flour, and you find them growing on ridges. And blue camas, a type of flower that shouldn't even grow in Alberta. I told a professor of archaeology about this and he said it was the northernmost he'd ever seen it growing, and that it must've been planted hundreds, even thousands, of years ago. The roots of the blue camas are sweet, and you can make syrup from them. They were highly prized. It was even used as a bridal dowry."

He speaks of the animals, mentioning that the area is rich with grizzly bears. "It's also the best elk wintering area. Two to three thousand come to the valley in winter. It's like something out of Africa. It's a place where you find plants and animals at the edge of their range. Scientifically, this is where evolution happens. Species are pushed to adapt! If you wipe out a species through development, then that process won't occur."

Finally, Bob speaks of the area's multi-millennial Indigenous history, and the horrors that ensued with European contact. "It was government policy to wipe out the bison to weaken the First Nations so their land could be taken. There are accounts of braves resorting to snaring gophers for food. By 1877, when the treaties were signed, all the buffalo were off the land. Once the buffalo were gone, cattle ranching took off, with cattle replacing buffalo, and the First Nations succumbed to smallpox. It was a holocaust for these people." This is the real Canadian history we are beginning to wake up to.

I ask Bob about how he thinks we, as people of the modern world, should approach Happy Valley. He says this: "Go for a walk there. See the hundreds of kinds of plants and animals. See how rich and vital it is. There's something fundamental going on in these places. It's in these places where we find...so much."

Grandma comes over to my house to finalize our travel plans. I take her jacket and place it on the hook by my front door. The faded green nylon is soft on my fingers from years of wear. (Grandparents who lived through the Depression were environmentalists long before present day. Grandma rinses and reuses baggies, and repurposes Styrofoam meat trays, well washed, as a bed for homemade oatmeal cookies.) We sit at my kitchen table and lay out maps. Then Grandma hands me an envelope. "I found this," she says mysteriously. "It's from your grandpa." It's an old letter dated April 13, 1999, addressed to me.

Apparently, back then, when I was in university, I was writing a political science paper on First Nations people. Grandpa had written the letter from his home in High River, saying he had many books on Alberta's Native history I could use. Grandpa was always curious about Indigenous history. During a stint living in coastal BC, he studied Haida art and would have my sister and I trace totems on cedar slabs, then wood-burn the images for our childhood art projects. He had a respect for what came before. His letter warns of corrupt government policies I might want to look into. Why hadn't he sent the letter all those years ago, and why am I receiving it now? It feels like a whisper, another map to Happy Valley. He's inviting me to learn the whole story.

I've often seen our prairies from an aerial view, flying home from travel. It's a patchwork quilt of property lines that makes me feel claustrophobic. It's so linear, so owned. The only thing that connects one piece of land to another is rivers and streams, which are "allowed" to flow through. I wonder if this is the current state of Happy Valley. Is there wildness left there, where the Rockies roll out to the prairies? Or has it been domesticated? As a child, I would look for hours out the car window on mountain road trips, willing myself to find a cliff so inaccessible that I would know, for certain, that no human hands had ever touched it. By seeing something in its natural state, I was returned to my own natural state too.

Imagine if humans and the environment could exist in a harmonious relationship. Where touching the land wouldn't automatically mean contaminating or altering it. This was how the Indigenous People of Happy Valley lived for thousands of years. In fact, they lived so lightly and with such respect for the land and animals that archaeological evidence is subtle. It's not like the grand pyramids of Egypt or the Taj Mahal. This is a signature of the ideal of Shangri-La – that humans find a sustainable balance with nature, removed from the craziness and neuroticism of the materialistic world.

Often, it seems Canadian history started about 150 years ago, when Canada became a country in 1867, or when European explorers came to a so-called great blank land of opportunity. That our country was new. These ethnocentric histories erase what came before. There is archaeological evidence that First Nations have inhabited these lands for millennia. Indigenous People touched the land so tenderly that what remains is often overlooked and undervalued. Unlike the grand pyramids, our relics are things like stone burial rings, Medicine Wheels, rock cairns, arrowheads, cave drawings and buffalo bones. Traditionally, Indigenous People were nomadic and moved according to the patterns of migrating animals and weather trends, and did not prize permanent structures. They packed up their buffalo hide tipis and flowed with the seasons. Sadly, over time, and with European contact and colonization, innocuous-seeming piles of stones have been moved – sometimes innocently and other times not – by farmers, ranchers, industry and government. The "modest signs of their passage" Liz Bryan writes about are being smudged out by time, graffiti and a general lack of knowledge about their significance. When these humble monuments disappear from the Alberta landscape, we lose our history, the history of those who knew the intricacies of this land's natural systems.

I've longed to learn more about those who came before the European explorers. Yet that knowledge has been largely sealed off in Indian reserves and left unwritten in the histories I learned at school. This land is the ground of cultural genocide. It's documented, has been thoroughly investigated and is an undeniable fact that our society is just beginning to grapple with. The impact of the policies of the Canadian government and its forefathers continues to cause suffering. I grew up amid a "Canadian" undercurrent of subtle and deep-seated racism. I have heard outright racist remarks about Indigenous People from the most unlikely people, as if this racism is totally acceptable. Many see First Nations in Alberta as lazy. Drunks. People who don't care about their homes. Let's be honest, it's a common Canadian perception. And it comes from the mouths of the otherwise kind people I know because it was unconsciously ingrained into them as children without their consent.

I wonder, after all that's happened here in Canada since Europeans claimed the land as their own, has the ancient wisdom that came before survived in the people? You see, the entire population of thriving, sustainably living Piikani people who lived in Happy Valley and beyond was reduced to less than 100 by the late 1800s. That tiny group was then funnelled onto reserves and into residential schools, where they were physically and sexually abused, their culture intentionally stripped to make them "un-Indian."

James Daschuk's book *Clearing the Plains: Disease, Politics of Starvation, and the Loss of Indigenous Life* describes the true story. He did an overwhelming amount of research into the policies of starvation carried out by the Canadian government. That's right. Tumble these words around in your mind until they sink in deeply: *policies of starvation*. (His book started as a doctoral dissertation at the University of Manitoba.) Daschuk notes that, in the winter of 1873–1874, Cree near the Alberta–Saskatchewan border were reduced to eating their dogs, and even their buffalo robes and moccasins.

How does culture survive that type of targeted killing? After all that was and is endured, is there a tendril that reaches back in time, or has it been severed? Where can I find the oral teachings of this land's first inhabitants? I don't want to learn their history from a museum or government plaque. I want to hear it from the lips of the people themselves. Problem is, I have no idea how to do this, or if it's even possible.

Webster Ranch, August 12, 2017

Grandma and I have questions, and we seek answers. Why is it called Happy Valley? Who named it that? What makes it happy? And what are its boundaries?

Bob Blaxley points us to Chimney Rock Bed and Breakfast at the Webster Ranch, where he did a writing retreat, saying the owners have good historical information. So that's where Grandma and I begin.

We drive south from Edmonton, then roll up in my black Volkswagen, now turned grey by the gravel roads. We swing the car doors closed, and the sounds of the countryside slide into our ears. All around are tawny foothills peppered with hardy tree stands. Sharp grey mountains rise to the west.

Tony and Deb Webster greet us. Tony wears a button-up shirt and has a relaxed walk. His father bought this land in 1946, and his grandfather came here to fish and hunt as early as 1906. Deb is wearing silver jewelry and her greying hair is pulled back. They invite us to sit on their porch to share their special view of Breeding Valley, part of the greater area of Happy Valley.

Grandma's oatmeal cookies break the ice nicely, and soon Tony is sharing tales.

Tony reaches for a stack of papers that includes histories written by his father, Art Webster. They explain that, in the late 1800s, homesteaders were encouraged by government officials to claim land. If they could sweat out the most meagre existence and "prove up" within one year (by erecting a sod cabin or some other little dwelling and not freezing to death over winter), they could stay.

Art Webster's writings explain: "The very name Happy Valley was in itself a misnomer. This was a community of very little co-operation, of constant bickering over land claims, and was named in contempt of the situation existent. Perhaps the geographical location, with elevation roughly equal to that of Banff (4000') with its frost and snow, which could come every month of the year, thus creating a mighty short growing season, did little to ease the frayed nerves and short fuses of those early settlers. The record of the numbers of hardy souls who filed for homesteads and very shortly abandoned same, portrays the difficulties they faced at the time. Many of such homesteads were simply incorporated into ad-joining leases, and now very little evidence remains of those early building sites. There were tough times in a rough environment."[4]

"Apparently, the reason it was called Happy Valley is because everyone here was so damn miserable!" laughs Tony. Not quite the origin story I'd imagined, but it certainly makes sense due to conflicting interests. There are tales of homesteaders being warned off at gunpoint in areas where the farming was good.

Nowadays, Tony and Deb are drawn to spending time on the land, and they strive to protect it. They're members of numerous protection groups, and their B & B was nominated to be featured in a *National Geographic* publication on geotourism. They ranch just under 1,500 acres of land. The weather here is extreme: Tony has felt a day start at -45°C and within eight hours it's risen to plus seven due to the strong chinook winds. The Livingstone Range is west of their land, and the Porcupine Hills are east. They are also near a Vision Quest/Iitáítsiiyiiso'p site called Chimney Rock. "We've been up there a couple of times," says Deb. "We've seen Native prayer flags there."

---

4   Art Webster, "1919 A Trip to Happy Valley – West of the 5th," from personal historical writings, 1976, 2.

She takes me to a corner of the deck to show me a pile of collected rocks and bones. One rock is encrusted with white shells and barnacles. The Royal Tyrrell Museum outside Drumheller dated the fossils at 400 million years, "give or take," Deb jests. Next she hands me a pounding or grinding stone, placing it in my open palms. Touching it launches me back in time. It's smooth, rounded, used. I don't want to put it down. I imagine squishing purple Saskatoon berries.

Their sensitivity to the outdoor world lets them point out elk on a high ridge, spot a beaver in the creek, and hear the many languages of birds. They have also spent much time in a tipi made for them by their friend Bruce Starlight, a Sarcee First Nations Elder. I wonder at Bruce's beautiful name. *Starlight.* The book *Indigenous Healing* by Rupert Ross explains that children are named based on their unique personalities and traits. It is the community's responsibility to nurture those gifts so they can be realized and therefore benefit others. What name would I have been given, I wonder?

The Websters clearly love the land. They offer to take us, complete strangers, on a drive in their Ford truck around the property. We roll along a well-worn trail into dense trees. Many have been rubbed by cattle, others by itchy grizzly bears. Deb scans the landscape for invasive weeds and notices the dryness of the earth. Tony drives the truck so gently I barely feel a bump.

We talk about the boundaries of Happy Valley, where it starts and ends. There are historical references in Tony's dad's writings that correspond with Grandma's, but they say the true Happy Valley has pliable boundaries – like a dream.

I think about their ranching life. There are no nearby hospitals, services or urban centres. It's remote. "It's not for everyone, this way of living," says Deb plainly. But to them, it's truly Happy Valley. They hug us and invite our return. As my Volkswagen exits along the gravel road, they wave until we're out of sight.

Grandma and I drive further south down Highway 22 (a.k.a. the Cowboy Trail) to stay at a B & B called Bedside Manor, located at the south terminus of Happy Valley and nestled in a curve of the Crowsnest River. It's a rural spot frequented by fly fishermen who practise catch-and-release. Resident roosters wander the grounds and let out their cock-a-doodle-doos, and my mind flashes to Nepal, with its own species of alarm-clock roosters and noisy, itchy dogs, to a time when I ate eggs laid by free-range hens. After scrambling them on cast iron, I'd wrap the eggs in flat chapatti bread made from wheat grown in the surrounding fields (harvested by hand, cut by scythe, placed in a mill powered by a stream and turned to flour, then formed into dough and fried on a stove fuelled by hand-collected wood and yak dung). There are similarities here. The fridge has milk from the owners' cows, and I pour fresh cream from a fat glass bottle onto my granola. Turkeys gobble about. Kittens jump in the grass. Laundry lines are stretched across the yard, strung with sheets and towels that dry stiff in the wind, then feel stiff on my body when I get out of the claw-foot tub. Their cotton holds the scent of fresh air.

In the camp kitchen, a fly fisherman named Herb approaches me. He's been coming here from Virginia for 35 years. He's 80 now, still spry. "Your grandma is really beautiful," he tells me with a grin, and notes that I could be that beautiful someday, if I keep it up.

He regales us with tales from his annual fishing trips.

"I've been fortunate to've been a guest in your country for all this time. I value the place and people. But to be honest, this place is threatened. There's a scarring happening, a scarring of the wilderness, especially along Highway 940." He's talking about a gravel forestry trunk road running up the west side of Happy Valley to the Kananaskis. Herb feels ATVs (all-terrain vehicles) are to blame. There's free camping, and people toss toilet paper and garbage into the streams. Their vehicle tracks eat up the earth and cause fires from hot tailpipes.

"I'm no tree hugger," Herb admits. "I was in forestry, and I'm friends with folks in the logging, mining, farming, and cattle ranching industries. But it all needs to be in balance. I see land being desecrated here." Herb wrote a letter to our provincial government – even though he's American – warning about what he's seen take place over three decades.

The bed and breakfast owners, Shirley and William (Bill) Sara, are doing what they can to protect the land. They're working with the Southern Alberta Land Trust Society to keep the water clean and prevent subdivision – a further dissection of the land. Bill, a physician and rancher (thus the hilarious guest house name Bedside Manor), strolls over to the camp kitchen and tells us that there's a sacred First Nations stone circle on their land, and that an oil pipeline was rerouted to protect it. And years ago, when a flood eroded a cliffside area, the family found buffalo bones, indicating a possible jump site. The owners seem to know the sacred nature of their land, as do their loyal guests. Grandma and I have found a good base camp from which to explore.

Voice of the Oldman River, August 13, 2017

Grandma and I drive north along Highway 22 to the waters of the Oldman River/Nââpi-iítahtaa, break west, follow its course awhile, then park in the dirt. Hawks and eagles stretch their wings to circle lazily over the ridges, landing in old Limber Pines, then returning to perch on fence posts. They hunt, watching with glassy eyes. We're going to see Grandpa's land, the place where we returned him to the earth.

We enter the Waldron Conservation Project, a partnership between the historic Waldron Ranch and Nature Conservancy Canada. A pact has been formed to ensure the land can never be subdivided or developed and can be enjoyed by future generations for its rich biodiversity and beauty. I follow Grandma as she picks a path through the dry grass. We're on the upper east bank of the river. There's a soft *sssss* sound as the wind gives the dry grass voice. A haze has thickened the air from rampant wildfires in British Columbia, and the sun shines through orange-pink. She's made numerous trips here over the years, but it's been a while. Her eyes spot freshly dug badger holes and the upturned little stones they've excavated with their claws. I find a rodent skull and place it in her palm. We touch the curving yellow front teeth. Grandma spots the three giant erratics that were left stranded by retreating glaciers. We orbit them slowly. One is cracked right down the middle, an ancient split. I see the patch of ground where Grandpa's ashes were offered and returned. Grandma and I don't speak. Instead, nature fills our ears.

We descend to the river, which the Piikani view as the source of all creation. For them, it was made by Naapi and called the Great One's Water. Jay Hansford C. Vest writes about their creation story in *The Canadian Journal of Native Studies*: "It is instructive to note that the Oldman River is located in the centre of this homeland which N'api made for the Piikanis, indeed, the river itself bears the name of the Creator...It is at the heart of an area which the natives refer to as 'Real Oldman Country.'"[5]

Did my grandpa know about this sacred geography? Or did he simply feel it?

The Oldman River/Náápi-iítahtaa rolls gently down its prehistoric course, held close by crumbling cliffs. Silverberry bushes shine in the half-sun. I find a fragment of hip bone in the stones, bleached bright white.

"Why don't we put it by the tree where we spread the last of Grandpa's ashes," says Grandma. She places it at the base of the tree and adds a green stone for good measure.

---

5   Jay Hansford C. Vest, "The Oldman River and the Sacred: A Meditation upon Aputosi Pii'kani Tradition and Environmental Ethics," *The Canadian Journal of Native Studies* XXV, no. 2 (2015): 580. Conrad Little Leaf gives the translation lihtsipāītsiiyiiso'p or Ksāāhkomm for Creator, meaning "mother."

I walk to the water and hop to a rock that breaches its surface. Dipping my hands in, I find that it's surprisingly warm. My hands, then my body, feel its very flow. It's not so deep, and through the water's skin I see colourful, smooth stones arranged on the bottom. The Old Man Naapi continues his endless polishing work, making them smooth, then turning them to dust. I feel protected here in Happy Valley in this curve of a lifeblood river. The surrounding hills have a burnished glow I've never encountered anywhere else on Earth. They invite me to roll in them, to become golden myself, to let go of the division humans create between ourselves and Earth and animals. I want to roll in them so deep that my body gets swallowed back in time, to a place before economies, domination, and the disease of stress and the illness of ownership. Grandma roams, child-like, amazed by all the little details.

Sacred geography is a fundamental ingredient of Native North American religious beliefs and practices. The idea of the sacred is founded upon a profound knowledge, understanding and conviction of the inherent sanctity of all things. Entering sacredness is the universal goal of all American Indian ritual. Their ceremonies are inextricably tied to the natural world. Portals to the sacred are the holy sites that dominate the spiritual and physical landscape of Native North American life.

—T.C. MCLUHAN, *The Way of the Earth*

Head-Smashed-In Buffalo Jump/N'inaa-Pissk'ān, August 14, 2017

Head-Smashed-In Buffalo Jump, land originally named N'inaa-Pissk'ān,[6] is a UNESCO World Heritage Site. Over 2.8 million

---

6 Conrad Little Leaf explains that Head-Smashed-In Buffalo Jump was the name given to the place when the interpretive centre was built, but that its original name is N'inaa-Pissk'ān, meaning the area where the

visitors have journeyed to where the agonizingly pancake-flat prairies buckle to form the Porcupine Hills[7] — the eastern boundary of Happy Valley. Traditionally, the area's First Nations/Niitsítapi[8] used the upward thrust of geography to their advantage. They created sophisticated drive lanes on the high land, then funnelled thundering buffalo[9] herds to the edge of a long cliff band. The giant animals would then plunge to their deaths below. The jump was integral to the survival of the people; prized organs and meat nourished them, and the hides sheltered and clothed them.

Alberta doesn't have pronounced landmarks like the Taj Mahal; rather, the original inhabitants here touched the land so respectfully that their legacy is more aligned with the leave-no-trace principal. One of our most visual historical remnants isn't a grand structure, but rather the skeletons of a major food source.

Grandma and I enter the interpretive centre. Five floors rise up the bluffs and offer museum-like displays. I have memories of coming here as a child and walking a trail at the crest of the bluffs. The view to the bald prairies was extraordinary. I felt like I could see to Ontario! But what really interested me was a sign at the trail's end. It read "Vision Quest," and pointed to sacred high ground off limits to visitors. In the past, young braves hiked there to spend four days and nights on the land in solitude, with no food or water. During their meditation they would pray to their Creator Iihtsipáītapiiyo'pa for a vision, which often came in the form of a spirit animal. I imagined their endurance, and how they must have felt communing with the earth and the beyond in such a direct way.

---

buffalo were processed, where the prized organs were collected, and then the meat, and then the hides (in order of importance).

7 The original First Nations name for these hills is more like Porcupine Tail, Kai'skāāhp-soy'is. There is a stress on the tail aspect, like the tail fanning out to form the hills, according to Conrad Little Leaf.

8 Niitsítapi, meaning "the real people."

9 Technically, they are bison, but they are commonly referred to as buffalo.

In 2014, Travel Alberta commissioned me to write an article about First Nations attractions in my province. I reached out to Head-Smashed-In interpreter Conrad Little Leaf for information, hoping to learn more about this mysterious site. During my phone interview with Conrad, I fell in love with his voice, how he spoke in slow, circular stories that curled and wafted like fingers of smoke reaching from a long-burning fire. At the end of our conversation, he hinted that there was some reason the two of us had been connected. The article felt like a drop in the bucket of all I hoped to learn, and so three years later the time has come to meet face to face.

Conrad greets us warmly. His hair is neatly tied at the nape of his neck, and two bushy sideburns creep down the sides of his face. He's wearing Wrangler jeans and a rust-coloured cowboy shirt with a proudly displayed name badge. I notice a stark resemblance to the Dalai Lama. Similar smile, similar compassionate outlook.

As a child, Conrad was tracked down by Indian agents, "caught" in his family home and taken to Peigan Day School (Roman Catholic), where he was beaten and abused by teachers and staff. Nuns made him memorize and recite the Lord's Prayer, and when he'd close his eyes and try to connect to god, and his words would come out slow and meaningful, they would yell and berate him, spit flying from their lips, and would beat him with a stick because he wasn't saying the prayer fast enough. He calls that time a brutal initiation, where they tried to get rid of the Indian inside him. He went on to attend Sacred Heart Residential School (also Roman Catholic) in Brocket, Alberta. His childhood friends did not survive, but somehow they knew he would make it, and they told him so. They were right. With all he has endured, Conrad still wakes up every day and thanks the Creator for being alive. He gauges the weather by watching the amount of fur growing on the local animals and the changes in the bark upon the trees. He became a secondary school teacher, and has a major in anthropology, a minor in art, and is skilled at linguistics. Conrad has worked at the buffalo jump since 2009. He is an amazing human being. If you go to Head-Smashed-In to meet him, he will welcome you like family and tell you the deeper story of his people. Conrad's spirit name is Piita Piikoan, meaning Eagle Being. He is Piikani,[10] a Nation grouped with the Kainai[11]/Blood and Siksika[12]/ Blackfoot to form the Blackfoot Confederacy, whose original name was Soki-tapi (flat/plains people).[13] Blackfoot traditional lands were bordered by the Rocky Mountains, North Saskatchewan River, the city of Regina – where the "berry people" lived – and the Yellowstone River in the United States.

Conrad isn't censored when he tells Grandma and me of the near annihilation of his people. After millennia of sustainable living, they were nearly wiped off the face of the earth by European contact. Conrad explains that the 80 million buffalo that used to roam Alberta were deliberately slaughtered in an attempt to weaken and starve them into submission; how disease (smallpox and influenza) ravaged them, wiping out tipi villages and leaving only a few children sitting with the dead, the glands on their lower jaws hugely swollen as they tried to fight off the foreign disease; how churches tried to convert them, breed them out and kill their culture; how the railway was built; and how Indian agents gave land to settlers, breaking promises and land agreements. By 1903, less than 100 Piikani survived. Of the new population at that time, only 5 per cent were Indigenous, the rest, European.[14]

This is not the story I was taught in school that focused on tales of brave explorers.

---

10 Also known as the Peigan.
11 Also known as the Blood.
12 Also known as the Blackfoot.
13 Conrad asserts that he is Piikani, not Blackfoot, and that Blackfoot is a grouping (of Piikani, Siksika and Kainai) and a name placed upon his people.
14 Daschuk's book *Clearing the Plains: Disease, Politics of Starvation, and the Loss of Indigenous Life* (Regina: University of Regina Press, 2013), gives much to consider.

Conrad shows us a black and white photo displayed on a wall near the front entrance. An Indian agent took it on the Peigan Indian reserve in 1923. A group of men gaze at the camera lens with baffled expressions, and I get the impression they've been subdued in a way they are struggling to fathom.

Conrad uses the image to tell me his family lineage. "My great-grandfather was called Āāpaiai-siksinaam, which translates as Weasel Black. They didn't like the translation of his name, so they opened a bible, pointed, landed on Joseph and gave him the name Joseph Little Leaf. That became his English name. And this here," he says, pointing to a man in the photo, "is my grandfather James Little Leaf [his original name: Mokaki'pokaa, Wise Child]." In those two generations, an entire world was decimated. The man in the photo before me bore the responsibility of collecting the bodies of his neighbours and placing them in a mass grave upon the rocks. He himself was so weakened that he couldn't hoist them into the treetops so their spirits could be free, as tradition dictated. The men in the photo are unnamed on the display, but Conrad keeps their memory alive by saying their names aloud and sharing their history.

"A lot of us died when the buffalo were wiped out in the 1800s. That was their plan. We had no choice but to agree to Treaty 7 in 1877, so we could get provisions to survive. The Blackfoot/Soki-ta-pi didn't understand English. We had no written language to read or sign any document,[15] but through an interpreter we agreed to peace and to prospering together – the settlers and us. The First Nations/Niitsítapi shook hands in good faith. We swore on a bible and smoked the pipe, and then they broke their promises. We never gave up our lands. Our land was taken." Conrad asserts that no treaty document was ever signed, and that what's often quoted

---

15 Conrad believes that Treaty 7 was written after the meeting of the Chiefs and the Crown, and that there is no signed treaty. He also asserts that there were no Piikani Chiefs present at the Treaty 7 meeting because they'd heard of Blackfeet First Nations in the United States being slaughtered by the cavalry and were fearful of being killed.

and displayed was written after the famous gathering at Blackfoot Crossing in 1877.

"Later, my people worked with a rancher to build a fence around a small area of land near Brocket. He was a good man, and he taught our people how to farm and ranch. But after his ranching failed, and he left, the RCMP forced us into that very area,[16] and it became our own prison. Peigan Reserve 147 A."

There is much dissent around the legitimacy of Treaty 7. Some Blackfoot people feel the promises made were never honoured. A university research paper by head interpreter Stan Knowlton/ Rabbit in Motion states that the Blackfoot have always maintained that the treaty was an agreement for policing, and that there was never anything about selling their lands. Some of the Blackfoot feel the treaty was fraudulent, and they want compensation for injury and all the lands that were taken from them.

And then there's the Indian Act, a piece of legislation written in 1876 that allows the Canadian government to govern most aspects of Indigenous life. A CBC news article lays out the hard facts: "In its previous versions, the Indian Act clearly aimed to assimilate First Nations. People who earned a university degree would automatically lose their Indian status, as would status women who married non-status men. Some traditional practices were prohibited. Between 1879 and 1996, tens of thousands of First Nations children attended residential schools designed to make them forget their language and culture, where many suffered abuse. On behalf of Canadians, Prime Minister Stephen Harper made a formal apology in 2008 to Canada's Aboriginal Peoples for this policy that sought to 'kill the Indian in the child.'"[17]

---

16 Conrad's father told him that, in 1952, the RCMP forcibly removed the Piikani off the bigger reserve.

17 Isabelle Montpetit, "Background: The Indian Act," *CBC News*, May 30, 2011, https://www.cbc.ca/news/canada/background-the-indian-act-1.1056988#:~:text=Since%20Canada%20was%20created%20in,band%20administration%20and%20so%20on.

If we dig deep and toil with reality, we find that much of Canadian history is neither honest nor kind.

"The Indian Act is racism incarnate," says Conrad. "I don't know why we condone it today. We're our own worst enemies. We've accepted the conditions. But *I* don't accept them. The children I see on reserve aren't treated as Canadians. Our children won't go anywhere. We're still living in the Third World here, Fourth World even, and people are dying. There are so many suicides. My friends say, 'I don't want to live here. I think there's a better place.' And when they have a chance they hang themselves. Doctors overprescribe painkillers and people get hooked. There are so many overdoses, so many deaths."

"You see, all the reserve land is not really ours," Conrad says. "We're subservient to the Canadian government, wards of the government. What we need is freedom. I just want the same rights as any other Canadian! New immigrants can set up a coin laundry, but we can't even do that on reserve. We get casinos and ring roads and wineries, but it's all a game. It's not ours. I can go to Calgary and buy a little lot and a house, and at least it would be mine. I can take pride in that! But I can't ask for a deed on the reserve."

"We need to stop this system. Get rid of it. But how do we begin again?" His question hangs in the air.

As Conrad shares stories, I feel it's not just him speaking. His ancestors' voices are coming through. Multigenerational trauma is flowing through him, and he's methodically ensuring his voice is heard. Conrad knows his views are not necessarily the views of the entire Nation – he's clear about this – but he wants to share his side of the story before it's too late, before the wispy fragments of the past are rewritten and buried completely.

I have a list of questions, as I typically do for interviews, but I'm quite overwhelmed by what Conrad is sharing. My linear questions aren't working in this situation. Conrad opens his heart, which flows up to his mouth, and stories wash out like a river of slow sound. When I interject with a question, it blocks the flow, so Grandma and I simply listen.

As I learn about history from another perspective, I consider the deep connection to the land and the aspects of his culture that have survived genocide. Connection to land. To ritual. To the Creator.

"Conrad, tell me about the land. What makes this a Happy Valley?" I ask when space arises.

He considers my question. Takes his time to articulate an answer. "This here is prime land. The Europeans came filled with greed. They staked out the raw land and became rich off it. You see, the land is the power. In residential school, they taught me about religion, but they never taught me about the plants, the animals, about Mother Earth. There were no female apostles. I always wondered about that. This was prime hunting territory. Elk, moose, deer, and there used to be antelope too," he explains. "There are wild turnips, raspberries, strawberries, onions; further up there's timber.[18] There are warm springs, and the water is clean and beautiful. Some of the species of grass are unique to this area, and that's why my people chose to live here. The buffalo loved the grasses. This place was a hub." I try to imagine a world where those ways were the dominant ones, rather than our current patriarchal/development-heavy/economics-based system.

I worry a bit about what Grandma thinks of Conrad's impassioned perspective, as her parents were settlers. She's been listening intently, taking it all in. Conrad spends a good part of our interview talking about the wisdom of Elders like her, and the power of women and their inherent connection to the earth. The conversation hasn't been polarizing; rather, it's like this meeting of cultures and generations is a chance to heal. Grandma later tells me that it's so important to see both sides – not just one perspective. "It helps us understand and preserve what came before." This meeting, this conversation, is *actual* reconciliation. By sitting and listening, and being in this sacred space together, we've bridged generations and cultures and met as human beings at a base level.

---

18   Piikani people are allotted a timber reserve called Peigan Reserve 147 B.

We've stayed with the discomfort of the past, roiled and sweated with it to understand it better. As white women of different generations, we are deconstructing our learned histories.

And I feel it. There's a healing.

I begin to sense that there's something else that makes happy valleys unique. To be within them is to be with the uncomfortable and unsanitized realities of our human condition. Like the species Bob Blaxley spoke of, the ones pushed to the edges of their comfort zones and forced to adapt, we too have stepped to an edge. And now evolution. Revolution.

Conrad walks us outside and takes a moment to pose for a picture. He diverts off the sidewalk and steps into the tawny grass. He's lit up by brass-tinted sun. "It's really sad," he says. "Our neighbours, the ranchers, they don't want to know us. But I'm ready for them when they want to change." Ah, that's why he looks like the Dalai Lama. His heart still has room for love.

Exploration

IT'S SEPTEMBER 2017: time for my annual girls' trip with my friend Amy. Amy and I met in anthropology class at the University of Alberta, and found in each other kindred spirits. Soul sisters, she says. Now we are mothers and live in different cities. Each year we make time to shed our regular personas and travel to a mountain location to be wild and free together.

Amy worked for Edmonton's Alberta Native Friendship Centres Association before moving to Kamloops, and because of her kinship with First Nations I suggest that this year we get into the mountains on the west flank of Happy Valley. We meet at Lundbreck Falls Campground, a provincial park facility on the Crowsnest River. We choose a sandy campsite close to the water and erect my tent.

Nearby, fish jump from the water to gleam for a moment in the sun – just enough time for the ospreys to swoop from the blue and pierce them with their hunting talons. It's a hot September long weekend, and the constant wind feels like a hair dryer on high. Fires are still burning all over British Columbia, and the sky shifts from clear, poignant blue to headache-inducing smoke haze.

Amy and I are quite similar. Similar education, interests and looks (5'2" give or take, blonde-haired, blue-eyed). She's even wearing a MEC brand tank I also own. We slide back into friendship easily. Amy is in the thick of rearing two beautiful young daughters, and this weekend away is a chance to reconnect.

We sit at a picnic table and pour wine. The sun sinks, the moon swells.

Perhaps it's the location, but our conversation moves to the topic of residential schools and turns serious. She tells me of how an Edmonton Elder she knew shared the story of how he was taken from his parents and put in boarding school in the 1960s.

"I remember him wanting to tell me his story," recalls Amy, her hair reflecting moonlight. "Sometimes the Elders would just open up and want to share. He recalled the trauma of having his hair cut (children were given short haircuts to make them look less "Indian"). Feeling the razor scrape off his hair." Amy is in tears now, as if she too is having her hair cut, her identity removed.

Some facts about residential schools: More than 6,000 Indigenous children died in residential schools and that number is growing as we find more burial sites. The odds of children dying in a residential school were one in 25 (the odds of dying in the Second World War, one in 26). Children were molested, raped and their bodies buried on the school grounds. One hundred and fifty thousand Indigenous children were taken from their families, and this program was in operation until 1996. It's unthinkable. It's true.

Amy knows the roots of this collective and individual trauma. The cultural murder and attempted assimilation of a rich, intelligent, sustainably living people. She knows it; she feels it. Her tears release it. But so many people are only just learning of it. The resultant multigenerational traumas keep a clear split between First Nations/Niitsítapi people and the non-Indigenous. Amy lets her tears flow, then we tuck into our sleeping bags and the river takes our tears away.

We are eager to get into the land. Amy invites her friend Ken Williams to come, explaining that he has a great knowledge of this area and people here.

We meet at the south end of the Livingstone Range. Car doors smack closed, and we introduce ourselves in a den of evergreen trees. Ken has silver hair and earthy skin. He's from Honduras originally, but when he first saw southern Alberta, he fell in love with the land and its people. He spent 17 years teaching Blackfoot/Soki-tapi students at an outreach high school and adult education centre. Ken was a competitive sprinter at the university level, and even raced Olympic athlete Ben Johnson. Now he uses athletics to bolster Indigenous youth.

We ascend a grass slope through wavy lines of heat. We crest a pass, and the wind comes alive. Its strength has been gathered from the ocean and is being exhaled with incredible force across the Continental Divide. It roars to our spot on the Livingstone and explodes east over the prairies. We have to widen our stance and hunch like cave people, or we'll literally be blown over. It presses my clothes flat against my body on one side, while fabric balloons on the other. We trip and stumble to a resting spot on the leeward side for a windbreak.

"Wind is connected to spirit," says Ken. In that case, we're getting blown clean, any mental cobwebs or confusion ripped off and offered to the wind.

I spot an eagle floating effortlessly on the thermals.

"Look!" I gasp. "It's holding something!"

Dangling from the eagle's talons is the limp body of a red fox. The raptor circles back as if to show us its catch.

We climb a knoll to a network of ancient earthen depressions. There is evidence here of the Clovis people dating back to over 11,000 years. This area was used to harvest chert, a type of sedimentary rock (also known as flint). It's a very hard material with sharp edges. Perfect for tools. We lower ourselves into one of the dugouts, and Ken finds some shiny shards. We touch them. Hold them. It's so strange, the juxtaposition of sitting in an ancient stone bed, contemplating what life would've been like so long ago, while above us a massive power line hums and sizzles and cracks with electricity. Nearby, we spot a box of empty shotgun shells from someone's hunting trip.

As we sit in the chert quarry, Ken tells us more about his life in southern Alberta. His cheekbones are high, and his face seems to always hold a slight smile, even when his mouth is relaxed.

"When I first came here, I wanted to experience the land more deeply. I learned to do this with the First Nations because they seemed to know how to connect with the environment." A Piikani Elder adopted Ken and initiated him into an ancient society, giving him the name Buffalo Runner. Ken has helped many youth with issues of suicide, depression, abuse and the realities of trauma that descend from residential schools. He had his own pain to process too, and decided to partake in a sacred Ceremony called the Sundance.

In the past, the Canadian government outlawed Sundances. Now, in our modern times, they are gaining popularity once again.

The Sundance is a powerful, emotional, sometimes seemingly violent Ceremony packed with symbolism. Men and women commit to four days without food and only tiny amounts of water. They dance and do rituals within an open-air lodge. In some societies, the dancers are pierced — men in the chest and back, women in the arms and sometimes the back. The warriors' piercings are then laced with rope or leather and connected to a tree, and their goal is to rip out the piercing. Ken was a full participant four times, and tells us about the experience as we sit in the timeless potholes, soaked by sun, dried by wind, breathing in the scent of sweet pine.

"On the fourth day, I was beginning to have hallucinations. Someone grabbed me roughly. It was my turn to be 'cut.' I was thrown down to the ground, and then I looked up to the centre pole. To me, it was now a real tree, and above I saw the vision of an eagle. When I was pierced, I had the experience, the real feeling, that I was prey being hunted by the eagle. Suddenly, I felt I knew every rabbit. Every prey animal. The hooks went in like an eagle's talons." Ken says he experienced compassion in that moment, the trading of life from one animal to another, and thus gained a deeper understanding of the natural world. Later on our hike, he lifts his shirt to show me his scars. A reminder of where he was "hooked." Ken was no tourist during the ceremonies, and because of his wholehearted participation, the Blackfoot/Soki-tapi now ask him to assist in Sundance ceremonies.

We offer water and pieces of beef jerky to the earth at the quarries, then head for the upper ridge. Ken looks to Amy, who is processing this place, so happy to be in the wildness. "When we come to a place like this," says Ken, "we touch what's wild within us. All this – it's inside us already, and being here reminds us."

When I was in Nepal, I learned that certain valleys have an associated sacred geography in the form of a deity. In the Himalayas, these places are called *beyul*. Ian Baker, scholar and author of *The Heart of the World*, writes about finding a beyul in Tibet called Pemako. It's seen as a female deity, and the land corresponds to her limbs, womb, breasts and heart. It was similar in Morocco with anthropomorphized place names. When Ken tells us that the mountains where we now stand are believed by the Piikani to be the spine of their creator, Naapi, I get shivers up my own. I'm learning that it's a recurring belief system, seeing the holy in the land. T.C. McLuhan's book, *The Way of the Earth*, explains that the Lakota's Black Hills are seen as a reclining female figure from whose breasts flow life-giving forces.[19] In our

---

19 T.C. McLuhan, *The Way of the Earth: Encounters with Nature in Ancient and Contemporary Thought* (New York: Simon and Schuster, 1994), 376.

collective human mind we pine for a connection with the land and see ourselves in it, sometimes in the form of a goddess, god or deity. When the world gets off kilter, it's the land we ache for. We want to see our physical form in it and feel we aren't separate. We want the land to take us back. We need to get wild again. Such is the importance of protecting Shangri-La; the earth has the capacity to make us right again. Yet the Black Hills, seen by the First Peoples as the *axis mundi* or centre of the universe, became the centre of a gold rush and were taken by settlers and prospectors. Trees were felled, gold extracted. The earth was seen by the new people as something to own, and she was treated badly. A question seeds itself deep inside me: What happens when we unwittingly destroy paradise?

We are exposed on the ridge, and the wind rips my sunglasses clean off my face. Twice. They smack the stone, and I scramble to retrieve them before they're blown off the ridge. This strong breath has shaped the trees into twisted, stunted sculptures, and their roots are nakedly exposed from erosion. We walk through a hallway of pewter tree skeletons. Amy takes shelter from the wind for some reflective time, while Ken and I push for the top, wading through the gale. We can touch the air. We can press against it. When we arrive, we find a protective rock bluff and hide behind it, soaking up still sunlight. My usual mind, always discontent, looking for what's next, finally submits and relaxes. I want nothing but to give, so I offer a prayer string I received from the Karmapa (the monk who will take over the spiritual guidance of Tibet after the Dalai Lama passes). I tie it to the distorted pines so the wind can share the blessings as it plunges off the edge, headed to eternity.

[In Blackfoot culture] women are stronger spiritually...they pick the sweetgrass, the sage, the berries, the herbs, the roots because [they are] closer to mother earth and therefore when they pick these things it is stronger energy.

Our hair is the grass on the prairie; our bones are the mountains; our veins and arteries are rivers, streams, creeks; our breath is the wind; our heart is in the middle of the earth...So for us Mother Earth is more than just a provider. For us, She's our teacher, our protector; we learn from Her...we heal from Her; if we feel like giving up, we sit on Her.[20]

—PAULETTE FOX

Amy and I rest at our riverside campsite and listen to the strumming of banjo strings coming from a temporary camping neighbour. It seems right that we are here together, two women breaking the river's skin with our toes to cool our feet, processing and philosophizing, then resting on a sand bed to dream. We talk about our dreams, our fears, our need to experience nature, and what happens when we're away from it for too long.

After giggling in the tent like little girls, we fall asleep. In the morning, just the two of us hike to a place called Crowsnest Cave. We follow train tracks that parallel the deep mountain water of Crowsnest Lake and come to a junction where the Crowsnest River feeds the lake, then look up. Water flows seductively over stone from a womb-like cave. We scramble up and enter the dark space. Inside, we find an exquisitely still pool of water glowing blue-green. As I observe it, I get confused. It's so clear I can't tell the difference between the bottom, the surface and the reflections of the cave roof. This is the river's origin point and is considered the genitalia of the Old Woman, the female Creator partnered with the Old Man Naapi. The "female cave" is the source from which the Old Man River/Náápi-iítahtaa flows, out past the lips of the cave entrance and into the world.

An old copy of *Hiking in the Historic Crowsnest Pass* says that the cave holds rare green and black Indigenous paintings, and

---

20   Paulette Fox, "Using Geographic Information Systems to Link Ecological Databases with Blackfoot Traditional Environmental Knowledge" (master's thesis, University of Lethbridge, 2005), 23.

warns that if they are destroyed, they are a resource that will be lost forever. Sadly, people didn't heed the book's warning. Curls of graffiti cover the walls, and though Amy and I search, we can't discern the ancient art. I suppose the graffiti artists were making their mark just as the First Nations did. However, by covering or removing the paintings, they helped obliterate endangered cultural artwork.

We return to our vehicles under searing heat. But mine won't start. Strange indicator lights are flashing, and though I just got it serviced, the engine won't turn over. My Google search shows that the area's only mechanic shop has just one star out of five, but there are no other options. I make the call. Soon a growling tow truck finds me. A man in his early 30s emerges. His baseball cap is layered with rings of dried sweat. His skin is a canvas for fierce tattoos. He sticks a cigarette between his lips and looks under the hood.

"I'll give ya a boost ma'am [at 36, I've become ma'am, which makes me feel old, but also safe because I feel like if he's calling me ma'am, he's less likely to get any ideas]. It'll cost ya $85 just to get it onta the flatbed, then $2.75 per km to tow it. You have AMA?"

Nope.

Amy and I scour my Volkswagen manual for clues. As we try to discern what to do next, a train roars by and the man literally jumps.

"Oh man! Whoa! That freaked me out! I got PTSD from the army. Holy shit!" Once he calms down, I ask him if he's getting any help for that.

"Yeah. I go to the range and shoot things. And get tattoos." He looks at me slyly. "Tattoos make ya look good naked."

Amy steps closer in an act of protection. Maybe this guy does like "ma'ams."

Luckily, my VW starts after several boosts. Amy and I bid the tow truck driver goodbye and depart for our respective homes. Tears in our eyes, we know we'll meet on sacred ground again, and that, as Ken reminded us, we're already wild and free within.

Immersion

The prophesies...state that the time will come when the White Brother will look to the Red Brother for guidance. Now we have to teach a world community about the responsibilities of humanity in a universe of alliances as we understand it.

—BETTY BASTIEN, *Blackfoot Ways of Knowing*

The following summer, in July 2018, I return to Happy Valley for the third time (three is my lucky number). I will become a shiver along Naapi's spine. I want to deeply investigate the sacred geography, to dive into the land and the body parts of Naapi.

Normally, I hike with my "Jane" perceptions. Now 37 years old. Female. Mother. University graduate. Great-grandchild of European immigrants. Product of a certain educational system. I'm imprinted with my life history. Now I seek an additional point of view, that of the Blackfoot/Soki-tapi people. History did not begin with colonization. "Canada" is not young. I have known this in my blood and felt the schism. This time, the path will not just be a physical hiking path, but rather an immersion into Naapi's world and the rituals of his people.

I'll be hiking with Ken Williams; the man Amy introduced me to in 2017 at the chert quarry. Buffalo Runner. I still remember the white scar tissue on his chest and how the Blackfoot invited him into their sacred Sundance Ceremony to help him heal his own human pain. Because of Ken's connections with the Blackfoot, I'll be granted access to attend a Sundance Ceremony on the Piikani reserve. Our plan: To attend the initiation Ceremony where a tree is cut, imbued with prayers and erected as the centre pole of the Sundance lodge. Next Ken and I will hike Naapi's spine from where the Oldman River/Náápi-iítahtaa slides through what's known as "The Gap." Ken sees meaning in this: We start our journey with the dancers, and then, while they're fasting and meditating, we'll be in the outside world upon the Creator's high ground. We'll be supporting them by being in the land. As a mountain girl, it's where I'm always drawn. I've told Ken I want to sleep up there on the spine. I have a strong need to rest my body on the rock and to have...time. Then we'll return to the Sundance for piercing day.

After bearing the suppression of their rituals, many Indigenous Peoples are now being drawn to Ceremony as a way to reclaim their culture and to deal with the intergenerational pain caused by cultural genocide. I wonder: As a white woman who is non-Indigenous to Alberta, do I have a place there?

Tree Day, July 24, 2018

I drive south down Highway 22, bound for the first day of the Sundance. But what am I doing? What will the Ceremony be like? Will I really be welcome, or am I just an outsider? What might I represent with my blonde hair and blue eyes? Do I hold responsibility for the tragedies that occurred deep down in my DNA? What does it mean for me to be attending such a sacred Ceremony? I'm tender and trembling as I prepare to take a big leap into another cultural world.

I feel my familial history as I drive, flanked by fields of wheat and bold yellow canola flowers. My grandpa's parents emigrated from Ireland, and he lived on Fish Creek near Calgary, which is now preserved as Fish Creek Provincial Park. In 2018, a new school on that land was opened and named Marshall Springs School to honour my family's history. After the celebrations were done, my mom took my sister and me for a hike through what was once her family's land. As we padded through evergreens, Mom recalled childhood memories of splashing in the creek, riding horses and spending days with her sister playing in the forest. She showed us a special spot where a natural spring gurgles up from the forest floor – thus the name "Marshall Springs." We were stunned by the beauty and this link to the earth, by our roots and our heritage, by the land that is now open to be enjoyed by all.

My grandma's side was from further south in Bassano, where her hands and the hands of her parents worked the dry and stubborn earth.

I feel sad. Why had this connection to the land been severed? Was it collateral damage that occurred through the so-called modernizing of society? My grandfather lost the connection, then tried for the last years of his life to buy Alberta land again. But he was too old by then. He got cancer and passed away in High River, never having quite realized his dream. I have a similar dream inside that has propelled me beyond the sod-altered city lots I've lived on to the far reaches of the planet. I search for wisdom cultures. I search for who I really am.

I'm about to enter the world of the Blackfoot/Soki-tapi to see if the traditional ways I've touched in Nepal and Morocco have survived within the people of my homeland. I seek their kinship. But after all that's happened here, what if I'm asking too much?

My cell phone vibrates against the seat. It's Conrad Little Leaf calling from Head-Smashed-In Buffalo Jump. At our previous meeting, he'd told me that many writers come seeking information about the past, but that few ever vet their versions for fact and sensitivity with the Indigenous People themselves before publication. I wanted to ensure my own interpretations weren't riddled with unconscious bias, so I sent him a draft of this book, and let him know about my plans to hike Naapi's spine.

"I read your book, Jane," he says, his voice like soft leather. "Your book, it's going to be good." He gives me time to process his words. He speaks slowly. "Now don't have any worries, any anxiety about your trip to Naapi's spine. You're already on this journey. I can tell by your writing that this journey, it's already inside you. When you go on your hike, well, it will be an unplanned thing. It will just happen, because you are walking the walk already. I can tell. That place is powerful. You'll feel the power of the Creator, the power of that place. You'll feel it in your heart, in your belly, a strong feeling."

"Take an offering of tobacco," Conrad instructs me. "You'll place it on the earth, or under a rock. You'll feel the power of the female energy, Mother Earth. You'll feel it in the rocks and the sky. Then say a prayer. Niitsítapi don't have written prayers; something might just come from your heart. Now you mentioned your grandfather in your writing. There might be something in your heart that's still wrapped up in there, something about your grandfather. So when you pray, think about him, your ancestors, your matrilineal side, your immediate family. You might have tears. Emotions. That's what it's all about."

Conrad continues, "Then pray that for the next 13 moons it all unfolds with ease. Like pages of a book already written that will just...open."

We end our conversation without saying goodbye (it's considered rude, better to say, "see you soon"). I exhale. Conrad has given his blessing. I'm not foreign. I'm human.

A couple of years after this conversation, Conrad and I will meet again on his people's land. He will speak of how the blood that flows in his veins is the Great One's Water. He will refer to all humans as being what's beneath the colour of their skin, beneath race. The elements. He will call us all relatives, all of us. He will light sweetgrass and pray and tell the Creator I am a flash of bright light that will share goodness with the world through my writing. For me to do such a thing means to ache with uncertainty, push every known boundary, cry, sit with darkness, trust my intuition and physically immerse myself in happy valleys and their mysterious ways. I must trust, even when I'm completely terrified.

I park my car at Ken's house and the two of us and his friend Tammy, who's been a teacher for 14 years on the reserve school in Brocket serving K–12 students, hop into Ken's vehicle bound for the reserve. It's been raining, and once we leave Highway 3 the unpaved road shines with slippery mud. We cross onto Mickey's land, whose family is hosting the Sundance. We descend a hill and pull into a field ringed by poplars. Ahead is the Sundance lodge, with last year's tree still standing tall at the centre. Surrounding the tree is a large, open-air arbour made by two giant, nested, horizontal wheels of poplar supported by pillars. I feel honoured and nervous to be on reserve land now. Naapi's spine arches up to the west, the Porcupine Hills/Kai'skäähp-soy'is to the east, and Highway 3 to the south. It's a pocket of preserved culture and landscape right within Happy Valley.

Ken and some others begin to strike down the old centre pole with axe blades. It is hauled to a private area beyond the arbour, where the Sundancers will soon be fasting. This tree will fuel a fire that will burn until the end of the four days.

A woman comes over to chat. Lorraine. Her skin is softly lined around the eyes, and her mouth droops slightly on one side. Her greying hair has been wrapped into a tidy bun. Lorraine has been a Sundancer herself and will lead the females. She looks me over. Stares me down. Notices my jeans.

"You'll need a skirt to cover yourself," she says, with a softly scolding tone. "You need to be lady-like." Tammy offers me her shawl, and Lorraine, without any shyness, reaches around my waist and ties me up, covering my female power.

"What other protocol should I be aware of?" I ask.

"Well, you can't be on your moon time." Menstruating women are seen as having extra power, and can even be harmful to the men. It's taboo to participate in ceremonies during this time. I've taken precautions for this: I've put myself on birth control pills in a way that will stop my period so I can attend (normally, this would be my moon time). She goes on to tell me that, once the Ceremony begins, no one can enter the eastern gate because it's the spirit gate. Altogether there are four gates that open to the four directions.

"Wear a long skirt. And no skanky shirts," she commands. Lorraine is the boss lady and the now-retired cultural liaison for the Livingstone Range School Division. Over the course of the coming days, she warms to me – a little. She will instruct me to share my snacks with the children, and one afternoon she will come over to my car to chug from my water bottle, wrapping her parched lips around the plastic rim and downing the whole thing before thrusting it back. She will also share tidbits of wisdom, while opening her slightly fogging eyes to connect deeply with my own.

Nothing's really started yet, so Tammy and I begin clearing brush from the old arbour in preparation. The arbour hasn't been sanctified yet, so we can move freely through the space. Suddenly, the sky opens and rain flows down in a torrent. I'm ushered into the driver's seat of a big pickup truck. In the shotgun position is Morris Little Wolf, and Ken hops into the back seat. Morris is the main Elder who will guide the Sundance. He's wearing a cowboy hat, and I marvel at this ranching world, so different than Edmonton. As we gaze through the ribbons of water rushing down the windshield glass, Morris talks about god/Iihtsipāītapiiyo'pa, how "god" is a name we place on nature, on creation, and that we are all part of it. "People get separated from nature," he says, his words rolling out really slowly. "But we *are* nature. We need to hear the stories. To remember. To reconnect with nature." He tells stories like the gravel roads of southern Alberta, each going its own way, then somehow coming back together to reach a destination. And sometimes there is no destination; it's more about the act of sitting together, and just – talking. We stay in that truck, where time has expanded somehow. What is it about being with Elders that feels so relaxing? I have nothing to prove with my words. I sit, and I listen, and Morris Little Wolf's stories within the cab of the pickup paint a world in my mind.

We are on reserve time (which does not correspond to clock time); and, finally, the tree Ceremony begins. Many more people have come, and we walk as a group to a poplar grove. Saskatoon berries hang plump on the trees. The rain has stopped, and there's a feeling of being in the prime energy of summer. A tree has been selected. Morris and another Elder named The Owl Talks preside over the Ceremony, and they sit down on chairs in front of the chosen tree. Men, warriors, are selected to share their own personal stories, and the tree seems to stand as a witness to their words. One man says, "Since contact, our people have struggled with alcohol. I, too, struggle with alcohol." He gazes at the huge poplar that will soon become the new centre pole of the Sundance lodge and places his worries upon it. "But, Ceremony, it helps. It helps me through." After sharing, he kneels before Morris, and his jeans press the wild grass. Morris prays in Blackfoot in a rhythmic beat. He has an eagle wing and paint. He dips his thumb into the burnt-sienna-coloured rock paint and slides it along the man's wrists, then across his emotion-filled face. Then Morris takes his storied hands, places them on the man's head, and prays. To see men feeling emotion this way, and honouring it, is moving.

The Owl Talks takes the role of explaining the Ceremony's meaning. He speaks to the group gathered among the swaying trees, and uses English words so we can all understand. The Owl Talks says it doesn't matter what colour a person is, because we are all one. Again, the lesson here brings things down to the human, or even sub-human, level in a gesture of community. I'm not excluded. They make it clear.

The tree receives a name: Sunshine. It was the name of the daughter of the family who is hosting the Sundance – she died of leukemia as a child. The crowd gives a communal "*mmmm, ahhh haaa*" of approval.

The tree has been chosen because it has a *Y* in its upper trunk, and this offers a particular symbolism to the Elders. "One branch represents the easy road, which is alcohol, drugs, entertainment. The other is the hard road, which is tradition and work," says The Owl Talks. "The easy road is easy at first, but gets hard as time goes by. The hard road is more difficult, but it's a better way and gets easier the longer you walk it."

Little girls dressed in skirts and headscarves strike the first blows to the tree. The Owl Talks explains it's because they are still so pure, and that the tree deserves to be taken by the most pure spirits. The girls take turns shyly holding the axe and touching blade to bark, assisted by a female Sundancer. As the girls take their turns, I watch the Blackfoot/Soki-tapi people in the trees. There's a mix of modern clothes and traditional. Many of the women wear headscarves. To me, the scene appears quite timeless. It's been played out over thousands of years. I'm witness to an ancestral connection to the land. I can hardly believe I'm here. And it's not exactly a jealousy I feel as I stand here with them, but a wish that I, too, had such deep roots.

Soon the massive tree is felled. A beautiful young man picks up a few textured shards of the tree and offers some to Tammy and me as a sacred token. When I thank him, he says, "Of course." He reminds me of Himalayan kids – skinny, spry, able, with dark hair and open eyes. Soon he will dance.

It takes many people to haul the poplar to the centre of the arbour. Ken has brought cloths of red, yellow, blue and white, and we wrap them around tobacco. We all tie our offerings to the tree, and then it is heaved up with a series of ropes. Old women feed the tree with prayers and with food. The tree has been planted and sanctified.

When it's all done, we're invited to Mickey's house. He tells me that he and his wife built it themselves. A huge table holds a feast of salads, meats and bannock. Traditional Saskatoon soup is laid out to share, and I dip my bannock into the cold purple broth and slurp as I sit on the wood floor with the children.

The next morning, I rise early and meet Ken. We drive north up Highway 22, that highway my grandpa loved so much that slides through the centre of Happy Valley. How different the trip would have been for Grandpa as he rode his horse over this land in the 1940s. He must have loved roaming like a cowboy.

We break west at the Oldman River/Nããpi-iítahtaa and arrive at the Gap, a prehistoric split in the Livingstone Range that cuts from river to sky. As children, my sister Shannon and I once exited Grandpa's station wagon to lean into the wind here. With our youthful bodies still light and airy, it seemed the chinook current was a visceral force that could actually support us.

Today, in the hopeful hours of morning, there is no wind. Just a faint dampness, a parting and opening of mist. We throw on our packs and ascend the first knoll to an ancient eagle-catching site. The site is a circle of layered stones two or three feet long and unimaginably heavy. In times past, this structure was much taller, but it's been toppled by time, or perhaps the stones have been taken. It's now open to the sky. The eagle catchers would have entered from the bottom to hide in the "chimney." The stories go that the catchers would place meat on the top to tempt the eagles. An eagle would peer down from above and spot an easy meal, tilt a long wing, then dive and land atop the chimney. The hidden catcher would grab its talons and pluck a few feathers. Then the eagle would be released with her food in a reciprocal relationship of giving.

Ken rolls out a buffalo hide and lights sage, sweetgrass, cedar and a special Sundance blend of dried herbs. We use the smoke to do a smudge. I love the process of smudging. You pull the soft, sweet smoke over your head, face, heart and body, with the intention to purify yourself.

"Now we're going to walk like the Blackfoot," he says, and our footsteps take on new meaning.

We climb up the first ridge. The rock is a steely grey and cuts my skin as I look for handholds. Ken pre-scouted a sleeping place a short way in where we'll set up our tents, drop extra weight, then press along the spine as far as we can.

We arrive at an upper meadow draped across the spine. On both sides the earth falls away. The meadow is peppered with massive boulders that fell off the mountaintop long ago. A strange mist has settled, and the place feels hallowed – a little like I imagine Stonehenge might be. I choose a spot in the shelter of one of the boulders and erect a one-person tent. I love it, this wild-style sleeping on the land. No campground, no rules and no one else around except for my new friend Ken. Ken finds his own solo spot. While he sets up his camp, I sneak away and find a boulder at the meadow's edge. A little evergreen has sprouted up beside it. I make my offerings as Conrad instructed. I offer tobacco, tying the coloured bundles to the branches. These boulders are mirrors of the ones at the valley bottom where we spread Grandpa's ashes. I'm in a meadow of timeless Grandfather rocks.

With lightened packs, we continue our ascent.

Ken thinks we should take a route to the right and then ascend a pass toward the spine. It looks like a good approach, but then the route gets hard. The slope becomes steep, riddled with loose rock over solid rock that causes our hiking boots to slide, slip and lurch. After a time, we decide going further would be foolish. We head back, a little disappointed, until we find a softer scree field.

"Let's go up," I suggest, and we climb to the crest of the spine. Now the going is good. The spine rises and falls in graceful undulations, and we cover ground quickly. Sometimes it's skinny, with sheer drops on both sides – a true ridge walk – to the point where it looks like we won't be able to continue on. But, somehow, there's always a way.

This entire region is Naapi's land, and his body parts enliven it. Stan Knowlton is an anthropologist, Elder, friend of Ken's, and the head Blackfoot interpreter at Head-Smashed-In Buffalo Jump. Stan has actually mapped Naapi's body in the landscape. Sacred places include the Elbow River; Nose Hill; Naapi's ribs, which form the Porcupine Hills, and indeed his spine; the mountains we now walk upon; and many, many more places with anthropomorphic names. Some of these place names are well known to Calgarians and the population of southern Alberta, but few know their deeper significance. Ken has set up a time after the hike for me to interview Stan and learn about his Naapi research.

As I walk the high land, the spine sends messages from an unknown mind like little pulses. Intelligence flows through the landscape.

We're high now, gaining elevation and distance. My spirits are high, and my pumping heart is clearing my veins. This is the type of landscape I love. If I were from a Clan, it would be a Clan of mountain people. My mom is at peace in the alpine environment, and I feel that high-altitude peace too. Up here, my worries dissolve and my perspective zooms out, way out, like a Google map. I get it up here. I like the big picture, the far-off views, the smallness of myself in this big, old place.

A strange mist sifts in from the east. It obscures and then reveals different views. Sometimes we see only evergreens and stones; other times we see deep into Kananaskis Country to the west, Happy Valley to the east and all the way to the Porcupine Hills.

We climb until we reach Thunder Mountain, at an elevation of 2186 metres. Ken finds a beautiful spot to rest, and I walk a bit further up to where the mist rolls over the edge to plummet into the Kananaskis. The views are spectacular. Peaks zigzag throughout my entire field of vision. I place my body gingerly upon the rock and rest my own spine on Naapi's. My body relaxes against the shale, and I look skyward. I'm a tiny blip of flesh between the deep earth and endless sky.

We linger a long while. Neither Ken nor I wants to leave. We try at one point, only to return to sit in the sun a little longer.

My grandpa would have been ecstatic up here. When his family was young, he had tried to buy land in Happy Valley, but his dream was never realized. His parents thought it unwise to take his family to a place so remote. This latent wish sat within him and took up great amounts of mental and emotional space. When he was an older man, it pressed him to take off alone in his car to wander across these lands. Now I feel Grandpa with me. Not as a ghost, but rather I feel my own body and mind to be an extension of his. Somehow he is gaining joy from the mountains. As I absorb Blackfoot/Soki-tapi wisdom, and feel the land, it's like Grandpa is receiving some sort of benefit. That thing wrapped up in my heart that Conrad somehow sensed? Well, perhaps it was Grandpa's unrequited wish to set his roots here. Each footstep I take, where my boots touch earth, is for healing. There is no need to own the land. To parcel or fence it. Instead, I fall into it and become it. And, in my doing so, perhaps my grandpa's wishes are finally fulfilled. Down below, his physical body was consumed by fire, brought to the valley, then returned to the earth. This journey had begun long before my birth. Like Conrad predicted, there is emotion, but it's not sadness or even the persistent longing I so often feel. I unravel the familial knots that travelled from Grandpa to me and sit at ease.

Ken and I eventually return to our impromptu campsite. We eat handfuls of trail mix for dinner, and share oatmeal cookies my grandma sent for the trip. We comb the ground for dry twigs. Some of the old wood here looks like ocean driftwood. Ken expertly starts a fire in the shelter of one of the boulders, and we sit in its glowing warmth. I feel like we are cowboys, and that during the night we'll take turns fireside keeping guard against bandits and wolves. But, in fact, we have our cozy tents, and there's no one to be seen in any direction.

After leaving the spine, I make my way to one of Ken's favourite places in the area, Beauvais Lake. Ken trains and kayaks here, and does meditative walks around its serene waters. I find a walk-in campsite and pitch my tent. And then I realize I'm the only camper. At sunset I go for a lakeside walk and hear the distinct *harumph* of a foraging bear and the shaking of brush as she searches for ripe berries. My senses are heightened. I spend the night with open ears and hear the flutter of insect wings, the tiny stirs and slices of air they make. The high vibration of humming bugs. Little bird voices, unique by species and message. I am on alert. Is all the food removed from my pockets? Will the grizzly bear investigate my tent in the night? I think of Cheryl Strayed in *Wild*, and how she spent her first solo night on the Pacific Crest Trail on guard to every sound and noisy shift of nylon.

Nature is not silent, but at least she rests. The birds peter out. The bugs too. In the morning, I feel them, hear them come back alive, and the sound draws me from light sleep. With open senses, I feel attuned to nature. I think about the Sundancers. They have been praying, fasting, suffering. Today will be the ultimate test of their faith and endurance. I drive back to the reserve for the piercing.

The sun is a yellow globe boiling amid heat waves in the July sky. I see Tammy with her high-school-age daughter, and we settle together in the arbour. Four buffalo skulls have been placed inside the circle, and the bone flashes white in the high summer sun. They are lashed together by rope. A threshold of dried sage has been laid across the southern door.

A man walks around the inner circle, pulling weeds and tidying. The leaves of the centre tree still look very much alive and are adorned by all our primary-coloured offerings, the scene backlit by the open blue.

Ken will be assisting with the piercing today. He has gone into a protected area where the Sundancers are doing a Sweat Lodge purification in preparation.

Lorraine heads over to chat with us. She's in her element, wearing a white blouse and a cotton, horse-print skirt with glossy ribbons sewn at the bottom hem. A braided tendril skims her back. She instructs us about what we will witness.

"There's a lot of anxiety today," Lorraine says. "It's a hard day for the dancers. They need strength. So you pray to the Creator, and as they dance, you give your prayers to the tree. Strong emotions might come. Your own emotions. It may be that you yourself are dealing with something. Just let go and give your emotions to the tree."

Lorraine gazes deeply into my eyes. She's teaching me. Good thing I didn't wear my skanky shirt.

The dancers enter. They are wearing headbands of rolled red cloth. The men are shirtless and wear red skirts. Their bellies are a little plump, their skin a little soft. The women wear headscarves and long skirts. There is thick anticipation in the air. A boy of about 12 comes to the onlookers with a tin can of smouldering sage. He offers the smoke, and I pull it over me. My eyes sting, and the smell of sage permeates everything, wafts over everything, and sometimes I'm not in Alberta anymore but am transported to Tibet and Nepal. The sage ignites flashbacks of cold monasteries where juniper boughs were lit and offered up to the Buddhas. The smell is so familiar, the act of offering so sweet. I've longed to touch this wisdom in my own country, my own province of Alberta. Yet, sadly, it was easier to fly to Asia than to carve a path into the reserves of my homeland. But, finally, I'm here.

The piercing begins. A man approaches the centre pole. Forehead touches bark and he yokes its strength. His back and chest are swabbed with iodine, skin is pinched, then silver scalpel slices through. A shard of wood is pressed through the resultant incision, so that it sticks out on both sides, a tense band of flesh still holding at the middle. When his four piercings are done, he is fanned with an eagle wing. Rope is tied to the two pectoral piercings, attaching him to the centre pole. He leans back, and the flesh of his chest pulls into taught triangles. With only air behind him, his chest, his heart, is pulled toward the tree. Blood stains skin as more dancers are pierced and connected.

Again more smudging. The boy walks clockwise around the arbour. Vigilant cleansing. Not only does this space smell of sage – my hair, my sun-warmed skin, the fibres of my long skirt – my whole being has become herbal and elemental.

After the piercings are complete, the Ceremony reaches fever pitch. The men blow high-pitched eagle whistles to direct their pain. They are all attached to the tree now. They move toward it, take deep breaths, then run backwards as fast as they can to tear the piercing from their flesh.

A yelp of pain as one of the dancers breaks free. Released, he runs around the arbour in celebration. The others must repeat the process until they, too, break free. Are they breaking free from their own suffering? Of the alcoholism they spoke of? Of abuse? Can the slice of flesh rip them from their personal inner turmoil? Finally, all the men have broken free. The flesh at their chest is messy and meat-like, peach in colour.

Now the back piercings.

Rope is attached to the wooden sticks that protrude from the back flesh of one dancer, then attached to the train of buffalo skulls. He begins to walk and the skulls drag behind. In the past, buffalo were food, clothing, shelter and pure survival for the Blackfoot/ Soki-tapi. Now they are memory only, but the dancers still actively honour them by offering their energy, pain and prayers. It is a balancing act of giving and receiving, an ancient contract.

The skin of his back pulls less than the chest, but turns indigo from the strain. He rounds the arbour, but his flesh does not break. He must continue until he bursts free from the burden. The skulls are kicking up a dust trail, bouncing and dragging like weighty ghosts. His face is determined but faint, slightly woozy, in a different realm. The skin will not give. Finally, two little boys sit on two of the massive buffalo skulls to weight them, and the flesh rips. He is free. He is weak from effort, so helpers offer support under each arm as he rounds the arbour. We step from foot to foot, dancing, transferring our energy through the earth, opening our palms to him. We spot an eagle in the blue, and he tips his wing.

Another dancer holds a staff with antlers on top and goes to where his family is standing at the arbour's edge. Among the family members is the young man who'd given me the tree wood chips on initiation day. When the staff touches his head, he breaks down and sobs. His mom's arms encircle him. To see a teenager experiencing the hot flow of emotion, face contracting and releasing in anguish, is an intimate sight. My cheeks glow, my heart buckles.

I decide to retreat to my car for a while to let my own emotions settle. I spread out a cotton blanket in the shade of the open door of my Volkswagen and watch grasshoppers play in the field.

An old man in a checkered shirt sees me and beckons me over. He reaches for my hand and the grip is soft – like a roll of fine silk. He's come from the nearby Blood/Kainai reserve.

"Are you a Sundancer?" he asks me. I'm surprised by his question. He has seen me as someone who could participate.

"No," I reply, and the sun spills on us in honey waves.

"Well, I'm here to support my grandson. He passed out yesterday and couldn't complete the Sundance."

I nod, and then he makes his way to the arbour. Perhaps the boy who was crying is his grandson, I think.

I'm not ready to return just yet, so I retreat to my blanket. I sit in the prairie heat and am swallowed by time, sheltered amid a field dotted with pickups. Another truck pulls up and parks nearby. The driver rolls down the window and starts chatting with someone sitting in the passenger seat of another truck. I try not to overhear their conversation, but there's no other noise to distract me.

"I don't know what happened. I just blacked out," says the person in the truck behind me.

"Ah, but you know you can do it," says the newly arrived man. "You've done it before. And you'll have the chance to again."

The puzzle pieces click together, and I realize the person parked behind me is the grandson, the teenager who'd offered me wood chips from the tree, the one who'd succumbed to the stressors of the Sundance. I now understand his tears. They flowed because he didn't complete his vow.

As they chat, I look to my rearview mirror. A mala necklace dangles from it, its 110 rosewood beads shining from the thousands of prayers I've rubbed into them. I'd taken it to the Potala Palace in Tibet – the former home of the Dalai Lama – as well as many great monasteries and sacred places. I'd been turning the beads between my finger and thumb pads on my anxious drive from Edmonton. An impulse arises in me, and I unhook the mala from the mirror and walk over to the boy.

"Excuse me," I say, as I awkwardly interrupt their conversation. "I heard that you're the Sundancer who was unwell. I'm sorry that happened."

He regards me with an open gaze. His head is shaved on the sides, the top part braided. I explain about the mala, that it's filled with prayers and has been to Tibet. I think about the wisdom culture there that has been forcibly colonized by the Chinese government, experienced fierce and overt abuse, yet is still strong in the hearts and minds of so many, including me, regardless of my physical appearance and heritage. I reach for his hands and place the beads in his open palms, then touch his hands as they close around the gift. He stands up, opens his arms and hugs me. He is two years older than my son. Later, his mom calls me over. "Thanks for what you did for my boy," she says. And I think, *thanks for holding the land, the animals and the wisdom for us all.*

I gather my strength and return to the arbour. I've missed the women's piercing. Tammy tells me that the women stood in turn at the centre while helpers ripped the wood through the bands of flesh upon their shoulders.

Now that the hardest, most emotional aspect of the Sundance is complete, each dancer walks in turn to the southern gate, where the sage threshold has been laid. They extend a hand or eagle wing and reach for family members, building a family chain to lead them to the centre pole. One older female Sundancer brings up her sister, and the two of them walk toward the tree. The sister's hair is thin, floating grey curls, and when she arrives at the tree, a slow wail emerges. It's as if the sound had been trapped beneath a heavy rock and is now being released.

Ken has been busy doing the incisions and piercings, but now he steps to the threshold. Who could he be calling into the arbour? Could it be me? Do I have a place in this Ceremony? As doubts and fears quiver inside of me, he motions for me to come.

Every cell inside comes alive, snaps to attention, begins to hum and vibrate like the bugs at Lake Beauvais. I instinctively remove my shoes and walk to the threshold.

"You are family," says Ken, and he takes my hand. We walk to the tree, and I touch my forehead to its soft bark as I've instinctively done with rocks and trees when I've been moved on my world travels. What I feel in that moment of contact is intense and unexpected. I experience the pain and emotion of the Blackfoot/Soki-tapi people in this Ceremony. Their fear, illness, hope and compassion are a flowing river. The Oldman River/Náápi-iítahtaa is inside me now. It washes through my heart, my eyes, tears slide down my cheeks, and then...I'm clean.

Thunder growls in the distance.

I drive to Head-Smashed-In Buffalo Jump, this time to meet head interpreter Stan Knowlton/Rabbit in Motion. Stan has worked here for well over a decade. He earned his undergraduate degree from the University of Lethbridge, focusing on geography and archaeology, and has served on the Piikani tribal council and fought for land rights.

Stan's ancestors have been part of this land for countless generations. His stories descend from ancient times. Elders told him that the Rocky Mountains form Naapi's spine, and then sent him on multiple Vision Quests to discover the location of other body parts in the land. He has used this information to build an anthropomorphic map that shows how Naapi's body overlays the landscape. Because of what I'd learned of how Indigenous Peoples of the happy valleys of the Himalayas and Morocco name aspects of the land, I was intensely curious to hear the Blackfoot/Soki-tapi perspective. What I was about to learn was far more in-depth than I could have imagined.

I'm led to a meeting room where several Blackfoot/Soki-tapi workers munch on snacks and chat. Stan enters and the room clears. He is a slight man with distant, shiny eyes. His hair is clean cut and short. He seems a little nervous. Or perhaps it is his nature; he shifts and moves in an almost pattern-like way. As a yoga teacher, I have the inclination to start our talk with some deep breathing to put him at ease, but, of course, I sit back and let things be. Our talk starts a lot like my talks with Conrad. Rather than me working my way through my list of red-hot burning questions, I'm launched into Stan's world of story, and it starts long ago. Stan introduces me to his ancestors as we sit in plastic chairs beneath fluorescent lights. He tells me about the movement of his family Clan between Yellowstone, Montana, and Rocky Mountain House along the Continental Divide.

"My people were the Spikskwi-tapi, the High Bush Clan. They were mountain people and had a different kind of life. It was harder up there in the mountains than on the plains and in the valleys. My people were warriors and the border guards of the high mountains." I'm instantly drawn to Stan's lineage for my own mountain girl reasons.

Stan works his way from his great-grandfather's time through a list of relatives, placing the names where they belong in the landscape and family line. At times, he pauses to recall someone and there is a silent gap. He is not only painting an image for me to know who he is, where he comes from and how he came to be here; this recounting of names seems to also serve to keep ancestral memory alive. He reaches into the depths of his mind to pull out a name, as if from a treasure chest. This action airs it out and brings it alive.

Slowly, Stan's stories come to explain the body of Naapi in the land.

"Everything around here is about Naapi," says Stan. He uses gentle hand gestures to construct the Blackfoot/Soki-tapi universe, as if it's being formed in front of us. "Naapi's playground/Nââpi-ot-si'ksikahtsiisp. Naapi and the buffalo. Naapi's elbow. Naapi's backbone. But it's not that simple. Names are hard to translate to English. Many names have been mistranslated, the meaning lost. The names are more like, *My elbow. My backbone.* As if Naapi himself is telling you those place names. This is my elbow. This is my heart."

"Ah, so it's like Naapi is speaking to you through the names?"
I ask.

"Naapi is communicating with you," replies Stan.

It is a common theme among places that came to be dominated by colonizers: The renaming of land. In the renaming, the original meaning is lost, and so are the stories that gave a place its name and power. So, in a sense, renaming places is an erasing of history and culture. As Stan tells me, history is a muck bucket of the conquerer.

Stan shares with me a list of place names corresponding to Naapi:

Kananaskis = Naapi's headdress
Sound Lake = Naapi's ears
Eye Creek Hill = Naapi's eye
Nose Hill = centre of Naapi's face (in Calgary)
Nose Creek = Naapi's nose
Lick Creek = Naapi's tongue
Rocky Mountains = Naapi's backbone
Elbow River = part of Naapi's arm
Hand Hills = Naapi's hand
Bow River = Naapi's bow
Little Bow = Naapi's arrow
Porcupine Hills/Porcupine Tail Hills = Naapi's breastplate
    and chest
Chief Mountain = Naapi's penis
Blackfeet River = Naapi's feet, near Missoula, Montana
Old Man River = Naapi's alias[21]

Stan tried to create a digital interactive map of Naapi's body parts overlaid upon the maps we recognize today to share with the world, but computer platforms keep changing, so for now his project is on hold.

---

21 This list is derived from one of Stan's PowerPoint presentations, which includes additional place names not included here.

In my research, I find another source describing Naapi in the land. Jean L'Heureax was a Montreal man who came west in the late 1800s and lived with the Blackfoot/Soki-tapi people. Way back then, L'Heureux drew a freehand map of the region.[22] "It is one of only a few maps dating to the 1870s depicting southern Alberta at a time when Euro Canadians were present in the country largely as traders, police or prospectors," writes Margaret Kennedy, associate professor of archaeology and anthropology at the University of Saskatchewan.[23] Her article in *Alberta History* magazine is rich with glossy map reproductions that illustrate a totally different Alberta. To me, they are like treasure maps revealing secrets hidden beneath our current world view. The most interesting thing for me was reading about the land through L'Heureux's words:

The descendant of Napa...the Blackfeet Indians, which for centuries have been the aboriginal population of the third prairie steppe, have a curious tradition...attached to the naming of the rivers and principal land marks of the great tertiary plain extending from the North Saskatchewan river to the Black Hills of Yellowstone valley in the south...The Indian nomenclature is supposed to trace on the soil the gigantic figure of a warrior in a crouching position, his face turned toward the Mountain ranges with arms in his hand and surrounded by all sorts of animals and birds etc. So we have such aboriginal names as the Head, the eye, the ear, the heart, the nose, the Elbow, the hand, the Bow, arrows and war club and the belly.[24]

During our chat, Stan also tells me of a prophecy marked on the Crowsnest Cave walls where Amy and I climbed the previous summer.

---

22 The map is held within the Arthur Silver Morton collection at the University of Saskatchewan Archives and Special Collections.
23 Margaret Kennedy, "A Map and Partial Manuscript of Blackfoot Country," *Alberta History* 62, no. 3 (Summer 2014): 11.
24 Kennedy, 12.

"There used to be a carving there. It's probably gone. I was there a long time ago. I could see the carvings then. There were two slashes across an image of Naapi's river. Now let me tell you the story. In 1923, the first dam was built on Naapi's river. A second one was built in 1992 – the Oldman River Dam." He says that the slashes on the cave carvings mark the locations where the dams were built. "It was a prophecy," he says. I think back to when Amy and I scrambled up the inclined stone to the cave but couldn't find any carvings or pictographs beneath the graffiti. The second dam, or slash mark, met with protest. It was built by the Government of Alberta to serve the dry farming communities downstream, but its construction led to active resistance from a Piikani group called the Peigan Lonefighters Society. The Lonefighters attempted to divert the river using an excavator, hoping to render the multi-million dollar dam useless and assert their connection to the sacred water.

Stan then speaks of a special healing place in High River, a place my grandpa loved to take us. In a bend in the Highwood River, two cottonwood trees once stood. They had a conjoined upper branch that made them look like a giant "H." The tree was seen as having great healing powers. The sick and wounded were brought there to be healed, and the dead were placed in the branches of the surrounding trees. This medicine tree fell in the 1950s in a storm, and a statue was later built to commemorate it. The area is now known as George Lane Memorial Park. Stan tells me that, after the summer prayers and healing were done near the medicine tree, braves would gather the offerings and take them to a very dangerous location, a big rock they called Naapi's heart.

"Naapi's heart is near Turner Valley [a little southern Alberta town] near the Sheep River," Stan says. "This rock was fed by natural gas and used to be on fire. Blackfoot legend has it that this place of fire spoke deep from within the realm of the Old Man. When the braves went there, they would be scared, because sometimes the fire would go out and the area would fill with gas. One little spark, and there could be an explosion or arc. They would carefully leave the offerings from the medicine tree at

Naapi's heart." It is said that, when the flame was reignited, a fire would sweep across the prairies, clearing the aspen trees, which would encourage fresh grasses that would summon the buffalo.

"Can you still see this place?" I ask, curious about the essential heart of Naapi.

"The rock is there, but the land around's been bulldozed, and the fire has been plugged up by industry. It used to have more trees around it and was a pristine place. I used to take offerings there. But now it's an industrial place."

My own heart feels a blow, then a tender blue bruising. I gaze at Stan. What can be said? The symbolic and physical heart of his Creator was altered with machinery, the blazing fire plugged and repressed. In that moment I know I will visit this rock one day to bear witness to what happens when sacred sites are damaged.

My trip ends like this: I have slept on a soft mattress at a bed and breakfast. Beyond, the road dead-ends at the new Castle Mountain Provincial Park. I'm supposed to drive back to the reserve for feasting and celebrations, but I wake up with my moon time. I'd tried to trick nature with birth control pills so my cycle wouldn't come, so that I would be allowed to participate in ceremonies, but it didn't work. Nature wasn't tricked. Somehow this feels deeply okay with me. I'm tucked away in solitary retreat at the feet of great mountains. I need time to process all I've experienced.

The owner of the bed and breakfast heads off for the day and leaves me in blissful isolation. Her property is stunning, filled with befriended hummingbirds whose wings sizzle through the air as they dart from flower to feeder. I write and write and write, and the words flow like blood through the body of a big, living story.

Around 2 p.m. I get a restless feeling. I can't sit, can't stay at my computer. The wild world calls me out one last time.

I go to Table Mountain within the new park boundaries. The trail sign says this is Blackfoot territory and orders that hikers leave any ceremonial items they might find. I begin hiking through velvet-skinned poplars alongside a stream. The deciduous trees give up and give way to evergreens, which in turn give up to become petrified silver tendrils. I almost give up too. This hike is hard, the ascent steep, and I'm trying to fit this in at the end of the day. But I find myself drawn on by the red desert-like rock. I could be in Arizona, I think. Finally, I find the top. I stagger to the edge of a 700-metre drop to the prairies. A 360-degree panorama opens up, and I see the land from a heavenly perspective.

I find a sun-soaked rock to sit on. I'm elated. High. Alone in my Jane-ness, yet part of this landscape too. I take a little lock of my hair and place my DNA under a garnet rock. My eyes try to trace Naapi's outline across the vast territory. Naapi doesn't speak to me with words, but there is a throb, a hum inside my body. I sit. I sit with it and smile.

Chris is the owner of the bed and breakfast where I'm staying. When I first met her, she came on like an avalanche of wrath about her frustration with the new regulations of Castle Mountain Provincial Park. As a long-time previous Banff dweller, she came here for freedom. She's from the Austrian Alps originally, has travelled the world, and has chosen to stay here. She hikes the wilds and ranchlands with her giant rescue dogs. She's not afraid of the cougars and bears they meet out there, but she does feel threatened by the park and its new rules.

"Tourism is as bad as colonialism," she says, as I drink coffee strained through her Euro-style, red coffee press. The new park is limiting her freedom to roam. With all the new visitors, ranchers are sealing themselves off so people don't trespass on their land. It's a hotbed, and she's mad.

"I've been to many sacred Blackfoot places in this area," Chris says. "I've found bundles [gathered sacred items]. When you see those, you DO NOT TOUCH. You back away. You leave them alone. There are some places we shouldn't go because they are too powerful. But if people come here without this knowledge, yahoos and idiots who don't know any better, well..." Chris wants to protect these places, but she's not impressed with what she views as the overcontrol of the parks system.

Once her wrath flows through, her avalanche, her fire, we realize we have much in common. She's Buddhist. She loves the land. She wants to keep it clear, clean and wild.

"Happy Valley is a slightly wrong name," Chris says when I describe my project. "It's not happy here. It's...well, it's about contentment. Life here is hard. Hail, wind, storms. But there is a spirituality. A deep contentment."

Later, she comes to where I sit and write on her porch, and she gives me a shawl made in Nepal. I hold it to my heart, and she says, "Even though you have blonde hair and blue eyes, the shape of your face looks Himalayan, I think. There's something there. Ah, you have Buddha eyes. That's it! You know the eyes you see in the paintings? Maybe you were from Nepal in your past lives."

It's not the first time I've been told this. Tibetans and Himalayan masters and friends have also said it. I quiver in the sun. An ancient story courses through me. When I follow it, it leads me to Happy Valley.

Naapi's Heart, Winter 2018

There is one aspect of Alberta's Shangri-La that continues to pull at me: Naapi's heart. The story Stan told me about how the eternal flame was plugged by industry haunts me. I think of my friends in Tsum, Nepal. Their culture has been protected between massive uprisings of rock and glacier since their historic migration from Tibet. But Tsum now faces the pressures of increased tourism and contact from a shared border with China. What will happen to Tsum's sacred sites? Will they face the same issues as ours, in

Alberta? Will Tsum's water be dammed for power, her minerals extracted for economics? Will communist China eradicate its traditions as it did in Tibet? Will the loud voice of the modern world drown out the whispers of the land?

I must visit Naapi's heart to bear witness. I ring Stan for more information, hoping he'll share the location with me. Together, we open Google Maps on our respective computers and he guides me to the Sheep River that flows through the 2,500-person town of Turner Valley. We zoom in to street view, and Stan directs me to the rock. It shows itself as a bulge of sedimentary riverbank that nature has heaved and folded upwards into a unique, heart-like shape. Behind sit two big silver globes belonging to the oil and gas industry. Abandoned industrial buildings punctuate the natural landscape. The earth all around the rock has been graded, and grey rip-rap lines the Sheep River to prevent flooding.

"It used to look nice," says Stan. "It was pristine. Now it's an industrial zone. I used to go there in winter. I'd go to a Sweat Lodge, and then I'd visit the rock. I'd park on the bridge, and from there I could see the flame burning from the rock's south side. There used to be a pilot light to prevent explosions, which was installed by industry. When I went, I would see lots of other footprints, tobacco and offerings. You see, these places, they give you energy."

"Did industry contact the Blackfoot before they altered the land around Naapi's heart?" I ask Stan.

"Oh no. And there will be denial all around. They should have seen what was going on there, but maybe they just thought the offerings were garbage or trash." Stan says this without malice, but with what I sense is deep exhaustion mixed with acceptance.

"At times, there was oil seeping out of the ground, and that had to be dealt with so it wouldn't affect the water. Then there was flooding. But no, they didn't consult us."

Stan doesn't go there anymore.

The area around Naapi's heart is unbelievably rich in resources. The land's newcomers came to know of this. In 1911, an oilman named Stewart Herron saw the anticlinal folds that form Naapi's heart and suspected they were signs of oil. He found seepages along the banks, took a sample, sent it to a lab in the United States and then quietly began acquiring the land and its mineral rights. By May 1914, a rig was set up. Soon a heavy flow of natural gas mixed with oil began to flow, and every few minutes it would shoot 50 or 60 feet into the air. This was the birth of Alberta's oil industry. At its peak, Turner Valley oil accounted for 95 per cent of Canada's oil supply. People in nearby Calgary went nuts, and within days there were 500 new oil companies. They wanted the oil, not the gas, so the gas was simply burned off. Just imagine: It's believed 750 billion cubic feet of gas was simply burned off. On the 2014 oil market, this was worth about $3.75 billion. The area became known as Hell's Half Acre because of the burning plumes that lit the sky. Development and industrialization: it seems to be the course of the modern world. The gas and oil find in Turner Valley created an unsustainable boom and bust system that we still live with today, one based on greed and economics that created a one-sided relationship with the land.[25]

Stan has been working tirelessly to document and protect sacred Blackfoot sites for decades, because over time many have been altered, vandalized or destroyed. "I've been to secret hidden places. But sometimes when I go back, I find that they've been destroyed. Places I thought would be around forever are now gone."

It's heartbreaking to think Alberta's cultural treasures are being forgotten and damaged, and that so few people even know about them.

"Stan," I ask, "this may happen to my friends in the Himalayas. What advice would you offer them to help protect their cultural treasures?" With a gentle voice, he replies, "Get pictures. Get as much info as possible. Document the stories. But, ultimately, it doesn't matter what you do. It's just like Naapi's heart, the rock.

---

25 Tony Seskus, "100 Years of Oil," *Edmonton Journal*, May 10, 2014, Insight section; David Finch, "100 Years of Oil at Turner Valley," *Alberta Views*, March 2014, 34–41.

It used to be pristine, and now it's an industrial wasteland. When something is going to happen, it's going to happen."

Pincher Creek, December 2018

Archaeologists have documented hundreds of First Nations/ Niitsítapi dream beds in southern Alberta. Just think of the beauty in that descriptive name: *dream bed*. These are Vision Quest sites marked by stone circles, where braves fasted in the high wilderness until they received their vision. Like Machu Picchu in Peru and certain structures of the Incan culture, the dream beds align their aspect with sacred mountains and star constellations. This wisdom comes from observing the sky, the seasons, and the movement of Earth and Sun. It is a language that the modern world has forgotten how to speak, a language that faces possible extinction and is held within the minds of extremely vulnerable groups. This trip, I wish to visit Naapi's heart, and it's also important to me to have my children and husband come so they can experience Happy Valley. My hope is that we can all learn from the Elders who still know this endangered language.

Some might dismiss talk of the Creator and Naapi and visions as fantastical, which would be an injustice. The relationship to the environment is how the Blackfoot/Soki-tapi people and other Indigenous cultures survived for thousands of years. They knew how to observe buffalo, seasons, stars, the ripening of berries. The land nourished them, and all was held in balance. In stark contrast to the "modern" world, which within only a few hundred years has almost murdered the planet. This is not an exaggeration. Let's look at the facts: The United Nations' IPBES (Intergovernmental Science-Policy Platform on Biodiversity and Ecosystem Services) *Global Assessment Report on Biodiversity and Ecosystem Services* is one of the most comprehensive reports ever completed on the topic. It finds that the health of ecosystems on which we and all other species depend is deteriorating more rapidly than ever. "We are eroding the very foundations of our economies, livelihoods, food security, health and quality of life worldwide," says IPBES Chair Sir Robert Watson. It's not too late, he says, but we are at a tipping point and need what he calls *transformative change*: "Nature can still be conserved, restored and used sustainably. By transformative change, we mean a fundamental, system-wide reorganization across technological, economic and social factors, including paradigms, goals and values."[26]

What if we listen to the voices that have been silenced for so long by greed and economics? Maybe there would be hope for my children and their children. The key to reviving our ailing planet may very well be hidden within the Indigenous groups of these happy valleys.

I plan for my children, Ben, now 15, Julie, 12, my husband Mike and I to attend a Sweat Lodge Ceremony with the two Elders who presided over the Sundance. The kids are learning far more about First Nations history than I ever did in school, and now they'll get real world experience being with Elders on reserve land and in Ceremony. I want my husband Mike to be in this with me too. For us all to connect, together, in Alberta's Shangri-La.

Once again, Ken Williams will serve as our bridge to the Blackfoot/Soki-tapi world.

We follow Ken to the Piikani reserve. Low winter sun slants hard, and its beams crawl across the dormant prairie grass, sliced intermittently by the spinning blades of southern Alberta's windmills. We turn off Highway 3 onto washboard gravel roads, then pull up to Morris Little Wolf's house. We step out onto the land and into the prevailing wind. An energetic dog bounds up and jumps all over us. The kids give it attention, and it looks up with

---

26   United Nations, "UN Report: Nature's Dangerous Decline 'Unprecedented'; Species Extinction Rates 'Accelerating,'" *Sustainable Development Goals*, https://www.un.org/sustainabledevelopment/blog/2019/05/ nature-decline-unprecedented-report/.

one strangely blue eye; the other glints greenish-brown. Its back is splattered with leopard-like spots, and it looks half-wild.

A growling fire burns in the winter light, and in its hot orange embrace it holds the rocks that will soon heat the Sweat Lodge. Morris and The Owl Talks sit in lawn chairs, along with a helper named Lucian, and in turn we shake hands in the soft style of the Blackfoot/Soki-tapi. It's more like slipping on a leather glove, the two becoming one, than individual hands asserting a greeting. The colours and textures of the scene from top to bottom are open blue sky, silvered fence posts and woodpiles, and dry golden grass poking through a layer of snow. The chinook roars through with unimaginable strength.

The lodge is surprisingly small. It's built in the shape of a dome, not tall enough to stand up in. "Come inside out of the wind," says Morris, and he leads us in. Morris crawls to the west side to find his place of honour beside an altar that holds an eagle wing, drums, a rattle, a pipe, and piles of dried sage and other medicines, carefully arranged. The other men line one side, while Julie, Ben and I sit on the other, organizing ourselves on tan carpet that has been cut and placed on bare earth. The winds have accelerated to 100 km per hour outside, but the membrane of the lodge protects us.

"I invite you to feel comfortable in here," says Morris as we adjust ourselves. "It might be different, or feel a bit strange, but this place is for you to feel comfortable in." His words give us permission to relax. Morris takes time to explain the symbolism of the Sweat Lodge. Willow ribs form the structure around us, on top of which blankets have been draped to form a protective skin from the outside world. The willows represent the ribs of Mother Nature, and we are now inside her womb. We are with the four elements: The earth is beneath our bodies. Fire will come from the heat of the rocks. Morris will ladle water on the rocks – good, clean water, he says. And we hear the clean-cold wind, singing across the sky.

"The rocks that will come in, they have been specially chosen," he explains. "They are old rocks. They've been on this land a long time. We call them Grandfather rocks. They are coming into the lodge for a purpose, have been chosen for a particular purpose. The rocks sit in the fire and get hot. Then they come in here and will make you sweat. The pores of your skin will open. You see, every day we accumulate garbage, whether we know it or not. And sometimes we spread that garbage to others without knowing. In here, we let go of that garbage and purify. We get restructured in here. This time, you are not in your own human mother's womb – you are in Mother Nature's womb. Safe. You can give her your garbage, and she will help you. She will take it for you."

I'm struck by the strength and metaphor of Morris's words. My book is about how happy valleys, these earthly Shangri-Las, are places where we can retreat from the pace of the modern world to reconnect with nature and ourselves. Now here in Happy Valley, in this Sweat Lodge, the Elders are offering a method and a direct portal.

Morris takes hold of a ceremonial pipe and packs the stone bowl with tobacco. He turns his gaze to me.

"Now take this pipe and tell us the meaning of this sweat and why you are here. We don't really know why you are here, so tell us." They want me to state my intentions. I gaze at Morris a moment. His legs dangle over the edge of the empty pit that will soon cradle the rocks. His pepper-grey hair sits behind his shoulders. "First, say your name to the Creator. This is important – saying your name. Then state why you are sweating. You are speaking to the Creator." He hands me the pipe. The bowl is cool in my palms, the wooden stem long and gracious.

"My name is Jane. I'm writing a book about happy valleys around the world. In our lives we sometimes get so busy and forget how to be with nature. I want to learn from our Indigenous brothers and sisters. I came to sweat so that, as I write, I write well. So I don't make mistakes, or tell the story in the wrong way. I want to sweat so I will have a clear mind as I write. I've brought my family so they can share in the story with me and be connected too, so we can be in this together."

They respond with murmurings of *"Eyyy, heeyy, what you have said is good. Your words are good. You are doing this the proper way."*

The pipe is lit and passed clockwise. It is smoked by the men, who pull the exhaled clouds over themselves like a shower. I love watching Mike smoke it, his body wedged between The Owl Talks and Ken. It comes to Ben, and he gingerly takes the pipe. His eyes slightly close. He's concentrating. Then he touches the mouth to each shoulder. He's a teenage boy, and yet I see an open door within him that hasn't been sealed off. Though we are raising Ben in the so-called modern world, and giving him tools to survive within it, we are not forcing him into its box, we are not forcing him to think that way, or be assimilated into it. Ben hasn't formed the shell that so many of us do as we grow up. My goal as a mother is to ensure that shell never hides who he is, that he always has space to be wild and follow his intuition. This image of my son with the pipe imprints onto me; it's one I will never forget.

Ken sits by the door, and Lucian the fire-keeper brings in the glowing Grandfather rocks on the tines of a pitchfork, placing them in a shallow centre pit. Some are river rocks, some are lava rocks that look almost molten. Heat begins to radiate, and we shed layers. Soon the men are in just shorts, no shirts, and I notice the smooth and hairless skin of Morris and The Owl Talks. The scars from replaced joints. Julie leans her little body on me, the door closes and then all is dark. The only visible thing are the glowing rocks.

Morris's words slide through the black. "The lodge is a portal to another world." He begins to pray and sing in Blackfoot. The sounds are soft and ancient, yet alive right here, right now. There will be four rounds to the sweat. In the first round, he prays to nature and calls the coyotes, interspersing Blackfoot with English for our benefit.

Splash. Spsssss. Morris ladles water from his metal bucket onto the rocks, and the lodge fills with vapour. Now it is hot, so hot, and sweat drips from our skin. I feel Julie drop to the ground and cover herself with a towel. The singing gets louder. The drum vibrates through the rich, wet blackness, and we hear the shake of a rattle, the hiss of water on rock. Where are we? My eyes open wide, bulging to see nothing and everything.

Julie calls for the door. The heat is too much for her. It is promptly opened for her, and when it is, the outside light is so bright it's blinding. Have I ever seen a sky so infinite? Julie leaves to sit by the fire, and we return to the rounds. Julie has often had a tough time with small spaces. As a little girl, she would get claustrophobic in our tent and need to get outside. Yet she summons her courage and returns for the next round. As we continue, I feel Julie beside me, and my own maternal nature swells. She and Ben came from my body, and now, here in the Sweat Lodge, we are all returning to the womb of Mother Earth to receive her support.

Inside, we each have our own individual experiences. In the black we can't see each other's faces, tears, smiles. There is no external display of politeness. We are basic, our senses drawn inward. We see with different eyes, beyond the normal chatter and distraction of our regular ways of thinking.

The Owl Talks has a nature I'm drawn to. He seems to understand the needs of non-Indigenous people like me, and why this type of Ceremony can be important for us. There is a softness in his eyes and smile that puts a person at ease. Between rounds, The Owl Talks speaks of healing.

"Right now on my land [he's from the nearby Kainai/Blood Nation, the largest in Canada], we are losing four or five of our people every week. Some to drugs. Some to suicide. Some to old age. People ask me for advice, and I don't have an answer.

"Morris and I both spent ten years in residential schools. We were just kids. We went through hell on earth. Ken once asked me a question about my experience: *Did you ever get angry?* Oh yes, I did. At times, I wanted to kill the people who hurt me so much. At times, I wanted to kill myself. Somehow I got through. If I can get through that, it shows there's hope for everyone." The door is open, and the light coming through allows me to observe The Owl Talks's face as he speaks. I want to hug him, to give him love, or rather, to share love. This man has been through more than seems tolerable for any human being. He was tortured by those who felt their culture was superior, and all he held dear was purposely stripped from him and replaced with Christian dogma and physical and mental abuse.

"So let's pray for healing. Let's pray for the Sundancers who fast and suffer for the benefit of the community. You will see them in the lodge today. They are with us."

Conrad, Stan, Morris, The Owl Talks and the Sundancers are survivors. True warriors. In a system set against them, they are still here, singing, praying and showing us the way.

For the fourth round, The Owl Talks tells us we are about to witness something very special. He's going to hand the right to run a round to Ken. Ken has offered his heart and time to the Blackfoot/Soki-tapi people, and though he's not Indigenous to this land, he has been wholeheartedly adopted into it. Race matters not. Actions do. The Owl Talks takes the ladle, holds Ken's hand, and together, as one, they steam the rocks. Ken sings his first round as a leader while Mike shakes the rattle. For Mike, this is way, way, out of his comfort zone. I know his muscle-laden, squash player legs are screaming in this small space, tucked beneath him. Yet he's here with me. He's here.

What happens in the darkness of the lodge at the point when your mind goes where it has never been before can't be explained in words. What you must do, if you want to, are drawn to, is to go yourself and connect with the Elders. Go onto, then into, the land with them. Make it happen in your own experience, in your own life. See for yourself what it's like when Happy Valley truly lets you in.

After the rounds, we exit the lodge and feast together at Morris's house. His wife Betty Anne tells me, "Well, now you know where we are. You can return." We eat at their dining room table, and Morris looks through the window, then points out a mountain range called "Old Woman Lying on her Back." He shows us her facial profile, her skyward-pointing breasts.

The Owl Talks has to leave, so I walk to the front door to say goodbye. He opens his arms for the hug I yearned to have. Hearts touch.

Before we left for Happy Valley, I'd been sorting through an old file of letters and poems my mom had saved for me over the years. I found one I wrote when I was about 12, Julie's age. I'd titled it (rather inappropriately) "Indians":

> I want to be part of the ancient rituals...with the elders telling ancient tales. Let me be one with the earth. Let me tumble with the flowing rapids, never having to take a breath. I want to be wild, being with the animals or the water. The sun or the totems. But let me be with the Indians. Though I am white I desperately want to let loose with the wild dancing in the light of the fire, under the diamond sky.

I don't remember writing these words, but I realize that, 26 years later, my little girl dream has been realized – and that now my own children have been able to live this dream too.

When we leave Morris's house and pull onto the gravel road, an eagle rises from the prairie and flies alongside our car.

Back in Pincher Creek, Mike sleeps away the afternoon. At night, he sleeps a solid 11 hours straight, like a baby. Normally, he has difficulties sleeping. His mind whirrs and recalls the day, thinks about the future, and he has troubles breathing well. Now he rests deeply.

Naapi's Heart, Turner Valley, December 2018

We follow Stan's directions to Naapi's heart, the last stop on our family trip to southern Alberta. It is clearly visible from the bridge, an upward earthen thrust rising from the banks of the Sheep River.

I feel anxious and strangely irritated as we walk toward the heart. This place has a ghost-like feel. The industrial heyday has made deep scars, and now that the resources have been drained, the land looks neglected and sad. Near the arching sedimentary layers is a chain-link fence, topped by lines of barbed wire, and, beyond, a huge abandoned gas site. "It looks so freaky," says Ben.

Our group of four breaks apart to explore. The penetrating odour of natural gas hits us in a wave. My nose throbs, our own hearts jump and there is a sense of danger. No wonder the braves were afraid when they laid their offerings for the people.

I walk up a shrubby embankment to the top of the heart. I take out a tobacco offering wrapped in bright red cloth Grandma Joyce gave me. Julie comes running to help. She wants to offer it herself, and she ties it to a bush. We offer the tobacco for Stan and all those who are helping me on the journey.

Mike is feeling uncomfortable and unwell from the gas fumes and wants to leave. He makes a break first, and the kids follow. It's a strange place, both powerful and really depressing. I hang back to process why I feel so uncomfortable. This place should feel special, but it feels abandoned and unloved. Inside of me, I notice a shifting wind. Though I know I will become more enmeshed with this land and the Blackfoot/Soki-tapi people, something is propelling me beyond. This place is warning me of something, warning me about the other Shangri-Las that remain hidden or teetering on the brink of human destruction. I pad sadly across the bridge, dragging out my departure, yet feeling that this part of the journey is settled for now. Stan's warnings about the inevitability of destruction and the need to document replay in my mind: *Document as much as you can. Because when "development" is going to happen, it's going to happen.*

I email him upon our return, sending him pictures of the heart and Julie making her offering. He responds: "Absolutely wonderful. Sounds and smells like the eternal fire is getting ready to ignite again. In the old days, it was a blessing to make an offering without being exploded. The little one and you honoured the spirit of the place. The syncline [where the rock layers fold downward in a U-shape] is female, and the water at the base is your connection."

I let the blessings settle into my own heart, then turn my gaze to the Himalayas, with Stan's message loud and clear.

3

Kyimolung Beyul, Nepal
September–October 2019

Finding the Eastern Gate

He brought auspicious portents to the land
And increased the majesty of its inhabitants and the environment.
He concealed inconceivable numbers of treasures in mountains,
    rocks, and lakes,
and miraculously left imprints [in stone] for everyone to see.

—NGAWANG ZANGPO, *Guru Rinpoche: His Life and Times*

HELICOPTER BLADES SLICE the dense Kathmandu air. It is post-monsoon season. The pilot has been waiting for the clouds to part their veil so we can safely make our flight into the Himalayas. He presses the throttle and lifts the metal bird from the tarmac of Tribhuvan International Airport. We rise up, hover a moment, then roar up over the incoherent maze of Nepal's capital city. From this aerial view, the hive of low buildings looks like a sprawling Lego project.

We fly north into the foothills, sliding past green ravines and frothing waterfalls. On my past journeys to Tsum Valley, it has taken me a full day's drive over bone-rattling roads, then days of trekking to reach my most favourite place on the planet, for no roads reach my destination. This helicopter flight has reduced travel time to a mere 35 minutes, and before I know it I'm dropped at 3300 metres in the mountain village of Lamagaun, Tsum, near the Tibet border. I'm greeted by my friend Lama Pema, who is a Tibetan Buddhist abbot. He smiles and drapes a silky *kata* (traditional offering scarf) around my neck as a blessing. I'd planned on hiking up as per usual, but at the last minute he'd offered me an empty seat on his incoming helicopter. We trade places, and he disappears into the sky. I'm left standing in the dream world I envision so often from my home in Edmonton. *Is this real?* I've crawled through my closet door into another world; gone through a portal; straight down the rabbit hole. I've entered Shangri-La so rapidly my mind balks at the shift. Aside from the rapid helicopter transport, it has taken me 11 years to land at this spot. Over the past decade, I've travelled to Nepal three other times, and have studied the area's spiritual texts and the academic works of those who have done deep study into this spiritual landscape. I have crystallized layers of trust with the area's Buddhist leaders, so they will show me the way. I was given copies of what is known as the *Kyimolung neyig*, a document that gives instructions for how to access the secret heart of this Happy Valley.[1] During this time, I've fallen hopelessly in love with the people of Tsum, and spend much of my time longing to be connected with them, for my body to be in this chasmic crease of geography. I partnered with Tsum's local people to create a registered charity called the Compassion Project, which offers free health care and kindergarten classes to the villagers. If you could crack open my heart and see the emotional connections inside, you'd find Tsum's tendrils wrapped all around and through, pulling and lacing it together in the most tender ways.

Tsum is part of a sacred landscape known as Kyimolung beyul, Tibetan for Valley of Happiness, or Happy Valley. *Beyul* are a series of hidden Shangri-Las created in the eighth century by a Tibetan yogi named Padmasambhava. Ancient texts describe Kyimolung beyul as being in the shape of a massive lotus flower that blooms across this Himalayan region. This trip I will go where few locals dare, as I attempt to reach its very heart, the centre of the lotus, which is accessed through a treacherous side valley called Sarphu. The walls in Sarphu are so vertical and tight that even Google

---

1 A *neyig* is a place guide that explains where the hidden treasures are. It was copied from a *terma* (treasure) revealed by Rigs 'dzin rGod Kyi Idem (Rigzin Godem). Shared by Khenpo Tenzing Lhundup, of the Nile Labrang, and Yeshe Palmo.

Earth can't penetrate parts of it. The texts describe Kyimolung as a fertile place where rare plants and animals thrive, saying that if you plant a seed in the morning, it will be fully ripe by night, and there are springs that bubble from the cliffs that grant immortality. If immortality isn't enough, imagine that over 1,000 years ago Padmasambhava studded the valley with hidden treasures, such as spiritual texts, necklaces and the body of a Tibetan princess. If this sounds like an adventure of the greatest kind, it's because it really is.

I'm led from the helicopter pad to the entrance of Tsum Monastery, home of our charity projects. Sixteen of our kindergarten students stand waiting in the courtyard. I drop to their level, and one by one the kids approach, with faces unmasked, curious and shy, and they offer me katas. In the past, I have bowed down to masters. Now I bow to the children, the next generation who will become the caretakers of this valley.

I'm here with my guide, Tanzin Gyaltsen Lama. This is Tanzin's birth village. He is the Operations Coordinator of our projects here in Nepal, and spends large amounts of time volunteering to provide villagers with free health care and education. Though he had to leave Lamagaun as a child, due to the Nepal civil war and the need to access higher education, he hasn't forgotten his Indigenous culture and works tirelessly to connect Tsum people to basic human necessities.

We spend time in the classroom, watching the students as they sit on the floor in front of low tables.

"A! B! C!" one child yells, as she points to the letters on an illustrated chart at the front of the class, showing off her memorization skills. Then she does the alphabet in Nepali. After the lesson, Tanzin calls the children outside. He places a tricycle on the flagstone courtyard. A long row of uncertain kids forms, and they watch with suspicion, backs to the stone wall. Tanzin lifts up one of the boys and places him on the trike. The little one's face starts off stoic, shifts to neutral, then a glimmer of light comes to his eyes, and he cracks a massive grin. Soon they are whizzing around, and the lineup gains considerable enthusiasm.

"You have to get down to their level," Tanzin yells out to me as he grins and plays.

School ends at 4 p.m., and Tanzin and I walk some of the children home. A boy reaches for my hand, and holds it as we walk, squeezing the fleshy pad below my thumb. We walk through muddy fields, dodging puddles and animal dung. I feel it in the hollow of my bones: I am with the mountain people again.

I'm staying at the monastery in a room next to the clinic. In a few short weeks there will be a grand opening ceremony for the monastery, but, until then, this place is a major construction zone. At 6 a.m. I wake to the sound of phlegm being coughed up by the throats of numerous construction workers. This is followed by the voice of a lone singer warming up his vocal cords for the day. Then begins the bite of saws, bang of hammers and whine of grinders. Paint odour permeates the air, emitting VOCs at levels perhaps not legal in Canada.

I crawl from my sleeping bag and survey the room. There's a private bathroom, with cold running water and a showerhead protruding from the wall. There is solar power and multiple available plug-ins where I can charge my phone. There is even Wi-Fi. A fast evolution is taking place – this is not the Tsum I remember. On my first trip, in 2012, I went three weeks without a shower because there were none. Now I struggle to compute the rapid change. It seems like part of my mind has been left in the helicopter to drift somewhere high in the in-between sky. I need to climb back down into my body. I exit the monastery gate, searching for connection. Beyond the linear compound is the more basic world that matches my memories. Animal dung. Wise trees. Well-tended fields. And the mountains. Oh my god, the mountains. I'm confronted by their immediacy. The morning is clear, and the Ganesh Himal range displays its 6000-metre crowns before my eyes. The sheer magnitude makes my heart jump into my throat, and pulls tears from my eyes. I sit on a rock and gaze as if looking at an old lover, and I let Tsum wrap me up and take me back.

Tanzin fetches me for breakfast at his family home. I'm a little shy as we walk along the village path, trying to avoid being sucked into the wet mud. The earth oozes, made oily from rain and mule excrement. Somehow Tanzin manages to keep his khaki pants clean, while my hiking pants are already hopelessly mucky.

"How do you do it?" I ask him.

"It's easy! Walk with your legs wider apart!"

He opens a wooden door leading to an inner courtyard. This is where the animals stay. Then we climb a ladder to the second floor. We find his sister-in-law sitting at the cast-iron stove. Wooden benches line the walls, and the window bank is oriented east toward the river. This is a traditional home in upper Tsum. It's almost identical to my other friends' homes – just adorned with different family photos and decorations.

My brain is still functioning at Western speed, but here palpable gaps of time begin to open up. Time between sentences and chats; between sips of 3-in-1 instant coffee in my glass cup (also a new phenomenon); between bites of breakfast. I seem to have forgotten how to simply sit and eat. In contrast, Tanzin and his family are comfortable with the gaps. The words are few but therefore welcome when they come. The silence is not stuffed full, nor carved up by distraction.

I grapple with the immensity of being inside my own dream, now turned very real. Tanzin's kindness helps with the transition. He plays with his little niece, and gives her a plastic doll with sparse blonde nylon hair. Tanzin is 27 years old. His stature is short and brick-like. He has a gold stud in his right lobe, and his forearm is inscribed with an intricate tattoo of his mother. The best way I can describe his personality is to liken it to a popular hot drink: lemon-ginger-honey – with an added splash of rum. Tanzin jokes that the local *arak* (whisky) and Gorkha Beer are good for trekking, as they provide a "warm inner blanket." His personality has the same effect. He describes himself as a bridge that makes connections and gets things done. Tanzin and his friends installed Tsum's first ever Wi-Fi dishes, and they manage Wi-Fi subscriptions. He's an entrepreneur in a fast-developing country. "Nepal is a good place to be an entrepreneur. There are lots of things to fix and improve here," he says.

The helicopter bump has given me extra time to acclimatize to the altitude and prepare for our month-long expedition. Our group will consist of five people: Tanzin; two porters; my friend Ani Pema, who is a Tibetan Buddhist nun from upper Tsum[2]; and me. Ani Pema lives in a remote hermitage in the far reaches of upper Tsum, wrapped on three sides by the Tibet border. I stayed there with her in 2012, and we became fast friends. Not only will it be fantastic to be with another woman but she also has first-hand, local knowledge of Sarphu, since travelling there on a pilgrimage 12 years ago. Her group didn't make it all the way to the heart of the beyul. Now she will have another chance.

I decide to use this extra time to hike north to find Ani Pema. It will be a good chance to stretch my muscles and revisit special places and people. Tanzin and I gather a few essentials, then exit the monastery.

Before we are past the village, I spot a trekking guide I know named Dhawa. Dhawa's wife, Phunjo Lama, is quite a famous Tsumpa climber, having summited Everest and numerous other peaks. He tells us that she recently took a group to Sarphu, attempting our same planned journey.

"It was really dangerous," Dhawa informs us. Phunjo's group of four university researchers from the United States, Belgium and Australia made it to an abandoned temple partway in.[3] Dhawa fears this season's rainy weather will not be in our favour, and suggests

---

2 Drephuet Dronme Nunnery, also known locally as Dherun. Founded in 1236, by Lama Madun Reachen (1197–1265). Dates shared by the Nile Labrang of Tsum.

3 I have tried several times to contact the academics on this expedition through Phunjo, but have not gotten a reply. Phunjo told me their group made it to the temple.

we should have waited until October. My heart sinks. As Tanzin and I wave goodbye, I hear Dhawa give a big-brother-style warning to Tanzin: "Be careful. And take care of Jane." A ripple of disappointment and worry rolls through me. If Phunjo – who has summited Everest – didn't make it to the heart, what are my chances?

I know the journey to Sarphu won't be easy. Locals are fearful of it and avoid it, and few foreigners have tried. A Western woman from Great Britain named Yeshe Palmo made an attempt. Yeshe became a nun in the Kagyu lineage of Tibetan Buddhism, completed a four-year retreat and was the resident monastic at Thrangu House Buddhist Centre in Oxford. She took groups on pilgrimages to Nepal, especially to places connected to Padmasambhava's secret valleys, and in 1999 she travelled to Tsum to study Kyimolung beyul for her master's thesis.[4] At the time, travel by foreigners here was forbidden due to its proximity to the Tibetan border and the sensitive political situation. Yeshe tried many ways to obtain permission from the Nepal government, and even enrolled at a Nepal university to help her case, but she was still denied.

That didn't stop her.

She decided to travel under the radar with one of the head *lamas* (teachers) of Tsum named Lama Sherap Tendar Rinpoche, of the Nile Labrang.[5] Along the way, she had to hide from police by ducking into the home of a village Chief.[6] They were compelled to choose a difficult route during monsoon rains by hiking over the 5106-metre Larkye Pass to reach Sarphu, and Yeshe did all this while suffering from acute diarrhea and altitude sickness, travelling local-style with little comfort into wild terrain. My kind of woman.

---

4   Under the guidance of Khenpo Tsultrim Gyamtso Rinpoche; University of Kent at Canterbury.

5   *Labrang* are hereditary lineages, and their role is to protect certain temples, spiritual texts and structures. There are three main Labrang in Tsum: Nile, Ngak and Khangsar.

6   Father of the 17th Drakar Rinpoche, village Chief of Chokang at the time.

She followed a sacred script that gave obscure directions to the secret inner realm of the beyul.[7] She later had it translated into English, and used it as the basis of her thesis.[8] Even after all that intense work, she ultimately chose not to publish because she felt the information was too secret. Unlike the dominant male/mountaineering/competitive attitude of find, conquer, plant a flag and become an expert, Yeshe's sensitive approach appealed to me. So I felt great joy and responsibility when one day I opened my mailbox and inside was a padded envelope containing her thesis, the English translation of the place guide and her handwritten treasure map of Kyimolung. I felt like Indiana Jane. I instinctively knew this was no small thing. I told no one but my husband for years, allowing the journey to ripen in its own good time.

Yeshe writes in her thesis:

When I went there it took a lot of persuading to get a local guide to take me. Living there for many years just by the Eastern gate was Pasang, a local guide; he told me that he knew of one group, Japanese who had gone some years earlier. One of them had died. He himself had broken some ribs two years ago going himself...foreigners don't go there.

Generally going down this valley is seen as very dangerous. All the locals know about this place. Nuns from the Gompa Langtrang nunnery and some local people from Tsum occasionally go there. However, it is not a popular place to go for two main reasons: it is both hard and dangerous, and there is no functioning monastery to stay when there.

---

7   This neyig/treasure guide was revealed by the famous treasure finder, Rigzin Godem (1337–1408), founder of the Northern Treasure Tradition. Revealed at the cave of Zang Zang Lha Drak on the stopes of Dugdrul Pungpa in southern Tibet, near Shigatse, according to Khenpo Tenzing Lhundup, Nile Labrang.

8   Ani Yeshe Palmo, "Bayul-Kymolung: The Hidden Valley of Happiness. MA in the study of Mysticism and Religious Experience" (master's thesis, University of Kent, 2001).

Yeshe and I became friends over many conversations, and she recalled her journey 20 years prior, saying, "I had such altitude sickness. I was shit-scared. I walked over a moving landslide, and down one side it was a sheer drop. If I'd slipped, I would have died. I got terrible altitude sickness. My lips were sunburned and swollen, I had diarrhea, and we had to negotiate three checkpoints because Tsum was restricted and militarily sensitive."

She passed beyond what's known as the "Eastern Gate" to the inner valley of Sarphu, but did not reach the core.

"When I failed and got back to safety, I laughed and laughed and laughed. Because I realized then that the beyul was actually in my mind. Ultimately, travelling to the heart of beyul is a skillful method to realize the spacious clarity of one's own mind. Beyul is not about the end goal, but rather a relationship with the landscape. We can see just how we have lost our connections with earth through what we are now facing in climate change."

Yeshe has become my dharma sister, a yogini woman to share my Western fears and issues with, and someone who has seen and stepped aside from the unhealthy, male-dominated monastic situations in which many Western women find themselves. (Transporting a spiritual tradition from one country to another can have unpredictable consequences.)

After the Japanese group's and Yeshe's attempts, I know of only a few other foreign groups that have tried. Dr. Nikolai Solmsdorf of the Bavarian Academy of Sciences wrote an academic paper titled, "'Sojourning in the Valley of Happiness': Shedding New Light on [beyul] [Kyimolung]." Nikolai's paper states: "Despite warnings about its inaccessibility, I eventually received permission from the local religious masters to travel to the centre of [Kyimolung] myself. However, unfortunately multiple attempts to enter the Sarphu valley failed due to unfavourable weather conditions and thus an exploration of the supposed centre of [Kyimolung] still awaits realization by future researchers."

I reached out to Nikolai, and he kindly gave me the name of another beyul expert named Eric Fabry. Eric attempted the Sarphu pilgrimage in 2009 and later in 2018, when he made it to the abandoned temple. He also found the source of a river that he felt was very spiritually powerful. Eric has a friend who made four separate Sarphu attempts, but didn't reach the outer bounds of the holy valley.

According to Kyimolung's lamas, the holiest heart of the secret valley is a mountain called Tashi Palsang. This mountain breaches the sky at 7187 metres,[9] offering a pathway to Nirvana. It stands at the furthest tip of the Sarphu Valley, hidden behind a sharp turn that masks it from the view of only the most hardy pilgrims. It was summited for the first and only time via the Sarphu Valley in 1954 by New Zealand climbers, though the Nepal government does not recognize this attempt. It was attempted again in 1983, 1994 and 2000.[10] The New Zealanders named it Chamar, a name locals don't use or recognize. The failed expedition team of 2000 tried to access Tashi Palsang from her western aspect through a different valley, but even though they had the permission of the Nepal government, protective monks threatened to stone them to death if they tried to climb it.

And now here I am, Jane in Happy Valley, about to make my own attempt to reach the heart of Kyimolung. I'm not here to summit or plant a flag. I'm here to be absorbed. I will live, for a time, in a place where a few sinewy-strong nomads intermingle with the wilderness and know its riches. I will live, for a time, in a place where wild yogis have pulled treasure from stone and earth and found enlightenment. Something has ripened in Kyimolung's shared story. Tsum's lamas,[11] Yeshe and my own heart are telling

---

9 My satellite map shows Tashi Palsang at 7100 metres. *Wikipedia* states that Chamar (another name for Tashi Palsang) is 7187 metres, and there are other published elevations.

10 According to the UK Alpine Club Library's *Himalayan Index*.

11 Lama Sherap and his nephew Khenpo Tenzing Lhundup of Nile Labrang, and Dungse Lama Pema Tsewang of the Ngak Labrang all shared the sentiment of wanting to share Kyimolung's sacred sites and history with the general population. This is in some contrast to the past, where such information was kept secret in the monasteries, or simply wasn't accessible.

me that the time to go to Shangri-La is now. Even if it means being soaked by the late monsoon rains.

Tanzin and I hike north on Tsum's main trekking path, which has been open to foreigners since 2008. This is an ancient trade route between Nepal and Tibet, worn in over centuries by the feet of humans, and the hooves of yaks, dzo (a yak hybrid), horses and mules as the grain and rice of fertile Nepal is traded with the salt, and now Chinese consumer goods (especially beer and instant coffee), of the barren Tibetan plateau. Glaciers reach down from above, transforming their solid nature into liquid waterfalls that dive off cliffs to join the Shyar Khola River as it tumbles down the centre of the valley. The river is tinted grey, with glacial silt and monsoon mud.

We are in the unpredictable, touchy weather before trekking season begins. The foliage here is full, yet it seems to be getting tired, as if waiting to relax into autumn's dormancy. When preparing for our Sarphu expedition, Tanzin had done a big shopping trip in Kathmandu for supplies. The only freeze-dried food he could find was Korean kimchi and bibimbap rice and noodles, as trekking season has not yet officially begun. September used to be prime trekking season, with blue skies and stable weather, but climate change has forced the season into October.

"Water will be our big concern in Sarphu," Tanzin says as we rock hop over a turbulent stream. Tsum's main valley is strung with steel suspension bridges and reinforcements along harrowing cliffs and landslide paths, but Sarphu will be another matter altogether. No tea houses, no toilets, no bridges. It will be full wilderness camping, and we will need to be 100 per cent self-sufficient. We expect to meet only a few nomads, who will soon be leaving as the season switches to autumn and threatens to unleash snowstorms.

The main trail leads us to a large *stupa*, a spiritual shrine representing the body, speech and mind of the Buddha. It was built many years ago as an offering to appease the local mountain spirits.

Workers are busy making repairs; the stupa is ringed with scaffolding. In Tsum, several hereditary lama families called Labrang are responsible for the spiritual structures within the valley, and we've now entered the territory of the Nile Labrang. A construction camp has been set up nearby. I see an authoritative figure clad in rust robes standing near the tents. It's none other than Lama Sherap Rinpoche, head monk of the Nile Labrang whom Yeshe travelled with in 1999. Lama Sherap arguably has the most vast textual and oral knowledge of Kyimolung beyul.

We veer off trail, and there he stands, his grey, shorn hair and spindly goatee giving him the aura of a wise master. I bow down, and once he recognizes me, he invites us into his yellow tent marked by a string of prayer flags. Their primary colours flicker in the wind. He sits at the head of the tent, then cracks a Thermos filled with raw milk and offers us some, but the smell is sour and hits my nostrils like a wall. I politely decline and take his second offer of tea.

It is not our first meeting. Lama Sherap shared information with me for my first book, and more recently he recommended that I make this journey to Sarphu.

"Rinpoche,[12] we are on our way to Sarphu in a few days. Can you give us any advice as we go into the centre of Kyimolung beyul?" I ask.

He considers this for a moment in his serious manner.

"You need to make offerings every morning to make the protectors happy," he replies. "You must sing songs too." Tanzin and Lama Sherap use Tibetan to discuss what type of songs to sing and which plants to offer, and, luckily, we know that Ani Pema can recite the needed prayers. He talks about how the treasure finder Garwang Dorje pulled out small treasures from Tashi Palsang, but that the big treasures still remain there so the area can retain its power.

I am wary and conscious of the dangers of writing about a sacred place. What if too many people come? Is now truly the time

---

12   Tibetan for "precious teacher."

to share this information? Am I the one to share such information, being an *inji* (outsider)? Too often in Canada, Indigenous stories were written, rewritten and appropriated by the non-Indigenous with a ton of errors and misconceptions, and so I feel a huge sense of responsibility. I voice these concerns in the tent. Tanzin and I had already chatted about how trekkers and climbers always want to find the next hidden valley, or climb the next untouched peak, how humans push and push for more, and I want to ensure I'm not likewise motivated.

There seems to be an urgent need to share this hidden and precious information in the face of environmental devastation, melting glaciers and the encroaching presence of the Chinese border that is close to where we now stand. Lama Sherap's nephew had told me that information about Kyimolung was previously held in monasteries, and that now regular lay people need to know about it. "Your work will be a breakthrough," he'd said. Lama Sherap agrees. "I am happy you are writing about Kyimolung. There are only a few Tibetan books on the topic, and none in English. It is good to share." With this renewed blessing, I feel more at ease.

Tanzin and I arrive at a guest house in Nile village. We have learned through the village grapevine that Ani Pema is here doing prayers and will come meet us. In the meantime, Tanzin and I sip black tea, and I listen to his entrepreneurial ideas, which seem to always spring from a heart that loves Tsum. For example, Wi-Fi. He and a few friends learned about the technology and installed Wi-Fi dishes as a service to Tsum, with a plan less focused on economics but rather more with the intention to connect Tsum to the outside world. As a trekking guide, Tanzin is creating cleanup campaigns due to increased tourist garbage. Tsum was once pristine, but the effects of plastic pollution, water bottles and peanut butter jars generated by the trekking trade are beginning to make their mark. We ponder together, and I feel the huge energy that comes with being in one's 20s as he shares his plans and aspirations. Tanzin's ideas are big, his mind fresh, and he represents a new round of caretakers and innovators produced by this valley. All of a sudden, Tanzin says, "She is here," and my heart jumps with joy. It has been two years since I've seen Ani Pema. Her pink headscarf appears first as she climbs the ladder. She wears a lightweight maroon jacket over monastic robes. The rich pigment traditionally comes from wild rhubarb that sprouts from the mountainsides, and is imbued into hand-woven wool. Her skin is smooth, the colour of creamy coffee, and her eyes glint and shine. She's slightly shy as we see each other again, but beneath the shyness is a big personality waiting to pop out. Ani Pema has been a nun since she was 9. She lives in the oldest temple in all of Tsum, built in 1236.[13] Her life is dedicated to operating the hermitage, praying, meditating and collecting firewood and yak dung for cooking. Lama Sherap is her guru. I've known Ani Pema for seven years now. In 2012, I stayed with her, just the two of us girls at her high nunnery in the cold-clear month of December. From those remote heights, lifted up and away from the mass and weight of the everyday concerns of the valley floor and my Western world, I'd had an extraordinary time living so simply with her. We've been bonded ever since.

As we sit at the guest house and get reacquainted, Tanzin translates for us. Ani Pema knows some English, but for some reason she's leaning on Tanzin to share her message. He calls us sisters. We are similar in stature and age. Ani Pema decides to stay with us in the guest house tonight while we make plans for Sarphu.

Before bed, I climb down the ladder into the black night to use the outhouse. The courtyard appears to be moving. Bells tinkle, and there is the sound of shifting. I realize I'm staring at a pen filled with yaks. The guest house owner guides me through a sea of long, dark hair and big horns to the toilet. "Sorry! They have just returned from Tibet," he explains. When I'm finished, I push

---

13 Founded by Lama Madun Reachen (1197–1265).

open the door, but he is gone, so I bravely exit into the mass of animals, parting them with reassuring words (I hope!) to get back to the ladder without being kicked or impaled by their horns. I listen to the sound of the bells that dangle from their thick, hairy necks. The brass clang is clean. Clear. It is the background music of time spent in Tsum. This soundtrack comes from the necks of yaks and dzo, and from the stoic mules that bring goods from the lowlands up to these great heights, and from the strong and slight ponies ridden by the local people.

Ani Pema and I share a room. She stands up on one of the twin beds and does a few prostrations before tucking under her blanket. We are still a little shy, old friends with old memories, now about to embark on a brand new adventure. We turn off the solar-powered light and say goodnight.

But soon there's a loud clatter on the roof. Our ears open to identify the sound. More noisy clatter. We giggle nervously.

"Troublemaker mice!" she exclaims in perfect English, though, in fact, the noise we hear is big fat rats. "Disturb!" We erupt with laughter and perhaps a little fear, and our multi-night sleepover party begins.

Nile to Drephuet Dronme Nunnery, September 14

Five a.m. light casts the scene out my window in soft blue. From my second-story room, I am peering into the neighbourhood homes. The exterior stone courtyard walls have precious firewood stacked on top, and its woody flesh looks strangely orange from the rain. I look to the glowing slate rooftops (beautiful but extremely dangerous in earthquakes, like the ones in 2015), and on top of these familiar traditional elements I spot solar panels and one of Tanzin's Wi-Fi dishes.

Ani Pema and I decide to hike to her nunnery. I'm aware of the huge gift of time I now have. Had it not been for the helicopter, I'd still be slugging up the approximately 70-km approach to Tsum. Tanzin stays in Nile so Ani Pema and I can have some girl time. She ties up her flat-soled Chinese sneakers, I, my hiking boots, and we set off.

We hike at a fast pace, and it feels divine to be outside and unbound by walls. Tsum comes back to me with each step. My first trek here, everything felt difficult. Slower. More emotional, as I worked through a lot of past karma. Right now, we are light like birds (perhaps it's because I've left my pack with Tanzin!), covering ground fast. Ani Pema points out a tight valley on the left (west), saying there is a difficult route to Sarphu that way. Gazing up, I see a stone hut, layers of green, a cliff band decorated with lacy waterfalls and, above, sharp sub-peaks. Cloud shrouds the main peaks. This will not be our route, but it's an interesting side note for someone looking for an epic expedition.

Soon we see Mu Monastery, the last permanent structure before the Tibet border. From here we break west and climb up, following workers who haul long boards on their backs. It seems there is construction happening everywhere.

Ani Pema tells me they're working on her nunnery. In fact, the entire nunnery and nuns' sleeping quarters have moved. The *gompa* (Tibetan for "temple," or house of meditation) where I stayed on previous trips had been hit one too many times by falling rocks and avalanches. Workers dismantled it and shifted everything to a safer spot.

"The statues, one man carry on back. But big statue of Guru Rinpoche [Padmasambhava], four men carry!" she tells me. I prepare myself for the big change that has come to a place I've held very dear in my heart. Her old nunnery was the climax to past adventures. We climb steep, new, hand-cut switchbacks. The earth looks tender from its exposure to the elements; juniper roots show off freshly naked skin. We overtake the workers. They are resting, exhausted from hauling materials up the slope. They tell Ani Pema that we are sisters with different noses. When she translates this for me, we smile knowingly.

Soon we reach the newly moved nunnery. The location is good; it is still high, with big views, and not in an active avalanche path. The nuns' quarters are in a long stone structure, with interior walls that divide the sleeping cells. Additional workers are carrying massive slate shingles on their backs in a sort of wooden backpack they've fashioned. Their calf muscles bulge with throbbing blue veins from the immense weight.

Ani Pema leads me to a temporary room she's sharing with another nun until her room is finished. There are no other nuns here now, as they are in the villages performing rituals. She pulls out a key and opens the lock on her door, and we step inside the dark room. I take a low cushion while Ani Pema sets about lighting a fire in the metal stove. The pipe is not yet attached, so she keeps the door open for ventilation. She begins to break apart juniper boughs and lights some bark. Grey light streams in from the door and crosses her face. I'm struck by her beauty as she crouches by the stove. Her cheekbones are angular and high, her teeth straight and white, as if she's had braces, her smile genuine and elegant, and her chestnut eyes reveal everything.

"Noodles?" she asks. I nod hungrily.

The workers smell the fire and begin to think of food too. One by one they come to her door to make small talk.

"They hungry," she tells me, but shoos them off. Now there is water in a kettle, and she's chopping garlic, then dropping it into a small metal pot to splutter in oil. It smells divine. Next an elderly couple appears at her door. She invites them in, and I scooch over. Ani Pema uses the kettle water to offer them instant coffee. They drink, leave, a little more progress is made on our soup, but more people come by, and she's inclined to use the kettle water to offer more coffee. This happens several times. Ani Pema doesn't seem put out by the constant interruption, and I notice there's a reciprocal, unspoken trade going on. She uses her precious wood to boil water (only a few trees survive up here, and they are marked with cloth as sacred so they cannot be cut down), and she shares her supplies. After drinking coffee, one of the old women reaches across me and leaves three packets of coffee for Ani. There's the customary cultural back and forth, where Ani says, "No, no, keep your coffee," and the old lady says, "Yes, yes, you have it." Eventually, it is left, restoring the balance of give and take.

Finally, there's enough of a gap between visitors for our soup to cook. We slurp down the noodles.

After lunch, she shows me the new temple. It's very strange to me because it looks almost identical to its former incarnation. Everything from the salvaged hand-hewn floor planks to the intricate frescoes, statues and Buddhist texts flanking the main altar.

Ani Pema looks at me nervously. "You want go down?"

"No, up," I say, meaning I want to see the old nunnery. She looks worried. We hike higher, past protected junipers and a billowing waterfall, and then it appears. The old nunnery. What's left of it, that is. Leafy tendrils have crawled between the flagstones of the courtyard and into the gompa itself. It's being reclaimed by green. The roof is gone, and the walls are crumbling. We walk into the open structure, and it is completely empty of what it once was. Ani Pema eyes me tentatively.

"Yes, I'm a little sad," I admit to her. "But everything changes. It's more important that you're safe from avalanches." I swallow my tears. I have loved this place for many years. And yet love, like all things, changes. We go higher still, to the hermit cave of a great master called the 16th Drakar Rinpoche. This place holds special meaning for me because my Buddhist teacher is his reincarnation.

I am not a religious person, but I've taken on the spiritual practice of Tibetan Buddhism like the Himalayan people here. I've gone through my own version of stages of being a Western student: As a starry-eyed new practitioner, placing my teachers on pedestals, with big ideas and a wish to "improve" myself; then feeling the hurt of not quite fitting the mold; then forging through the desolate ground of practising alone after leaving organized groups, dogmatic institutions and spiritual politics altogether. And so, having waded through all this in a less than graceful way, I've found the best way for me to practise Buddhism is in a more yogic, less monastic way. Many great spiritual teachings from Tibetan Buddhism have migrated to the Western world, but unfortunately, in my opinion, so have many hierarchical and patriarchal structures. I have spider senses for big gurus on ego trips, who themselves have unfortunately been blinded by big donations and high thrones.

I chose a teacher carefully, and he is the reincarnation of the yogi who once sat in solitude in these mountains. The 16th Karmapa recognized him as a *tulku* (reincarnation) when he was a little boy in Tsum, and I've heard him called a "hidden yogi." If he wanted to, he could have a big monastery and money, and could travel the world at will. He's not a monk and quietly refuses hierarchy. He is a humble man with a ponytail and blue jeans, and he lives in a cramped, rented apartment in Kathmandu that he found after he had to leave his other cramped, rented apartment when the rent increased. Being around him is to be charged by a clear lightning bolt, and then to laugh about it. I feel close to him as I sit in the leafy cave with Ani Pema. She takes a video of me as I leave a small offering of wildflowers and a lock of my hair upon the wet stone.

On the way back to Nile, Ani Pema tells me she's considering doing a solitary retreat that will last three years, three months, three weeks and three days. I'm proud of her. So many of the nuns she grew up with have left the sisterhood to marry, or simply to leave monastic life. Ani Pema is one of a few who is naturally suited to this type of wild, sometimes lonely, regimented life. Yet she's a paradox. Having gotten to know Ani, I can say that her spirit is anything but regimented.

The weather is bad. Really bad. Water flows all around me. Rain falls from a steel sky, the snowpack shrinks and shrugs off volume, streams bubble and tumble over stone, and waterfalls seethe white. What if I've come all this way to be turned back by the elements?

Ani Pema returns to the other nuns to do prayers and will join us in a couple days to begin the Sarphu expedition. Tanzin and I set off for a place called Pigeon Cave/Piren Phu – also known as Nose Cave, because if you look up the cliff where it is situated, its openings look like nostrils. Again, I wonder at the anthropomorphizing of the land. In the stony fastness above the villages, it is believed that a wild yogi named Milarepa meditated there in the 11th century. Milarepa is one of Tibetan Buddhism's great heroes. He wandered the mountains like a madman, turning green from his diet of nettles, yet achieving enlightenment through these nonconformist methods. Ever since I'd first seen Pigeon Cave in 2012, I'd wanted to spend a night inside it. I've now found a sliver of time where my dream might come true.

We pass through the village of Burgi that rests between the Shyar Khola and the sacred enclosures. A woman spots us and beckons us into her home. She happens to be the mother of one of our kindergarten students. She makes us tea, and when she hears I want to sleep in the cave, she offers to hike dinner up to me. I decline, preferring my package of freeze-dried Korean food and solace. She gives us two brass butter lamps to provide light for the night ahead. In Tibet and the Himalayas, they use yak (technically nak, which is the female form of yak) butter and place a wick inside.

"You are brave," she says, and internally I wonder why she thinks so. We pop out her back door and climb up the mountain.

Tanzin and I reach the cave complex. Walls and doors have been built to enclose the front sides of the stony portals, forming retreat rooms and a temple. He opens the little wooden door of the highest sanctuary and helps me get settled. I am to hang the butter lamps from a suspended wooden lamp holder that dangles in the middle of the cave.

"Put them here," explains Tanzin. "Otherwise, the rats will eat the butter."

"Rats?" I ask. "Do you think there will be rats?"

He scans the textured cave walls. "Yes. Maybe."

"Will they...crawl on me?"

"No, I think they will leave you alone."

He surveys the room.

"Don't worry. There are no tigers or bears here. You might hear animals though. Yaks might be outside, or deer. But don't be scared." He does a final check to ensure I'll be okay, looks just a little bit worried, then walks down the path to leave me in solitude. I'm not scared. I'm thrilled! I'm going to sleep here like a wild yogini, alone in the mountain hold. I was nervous the villagers would prefer me not to sleep here for the night. Really, it's akin to sleeping in a holy tomb, or a museum exhibit that holds precious history. But such is the generosity of the people of Tsum.

Now I am completely alone. I sit on my sleeping bag and gaze up, letting my eyes scan my surroundings. Sitting before me in a depression in the cave wall is a Milarepa statue. He sits there cross-legged, right hand to his ear in a *mudra* (gesture) of listening, a wild grin stretched across his face. The cave wall behind has been plastered white, and a big circular rainbow forms a halo radiating around his crown. I sit and stare in the womb-like enclosure.

My hope: that some time alone inside the mountain will untie any knots inside me, and unite me to Tsum, preparing me for the difficulties ahead in Sarphu. Before the final sinking of the sun, I open the doors and go outside to absorb the view. Far below is a patchwork quilt of farmers' fields, and the big red roof of the Rachen Nunnery. A waterfall races down a steep course next to the retreat room. The water level is higher than I've ever seen it. Its voice is liquid and flexible, yet also commanding.

I re-ascend the steep steps, climb through the little red doors, then seal myself inside. I light one of the butter lamps and, against local advice, I place it on the stone ledge in front of the altar. I can't resist, because it casts the most beautiful glow upon Milarepa. A massive insect with at least 60 legs watches me from the windowsill.

Milarepa was famous for composing spontaneous songs during his mountain ramblings, and it is said that right here he sang to a small group of pigeons, who transformed into goddesses. Yeshe had sent me a recording of her own voice singing the Pigeon Goddess song, and sometimes we'd call each other and sing it together. It's about the practice of Mahamudra, a teaching that asks you to look directly into the depths of your own mind to find enlightenment, rather than seeking it outside of yourself. I begin to sing it at its place of origin.

The sixfold collection of consciousness [meaning our senses]
Is lucid right there in itself.
This is the nondual, perceived/perceiver not two
When this is pointed out.

I gaze at Milarepa as I sing. Sometimes his grin turns scary. Sometimes it looks like he's laughing at a hilarious inside joke.

From my journal: "I hope that tonight will prepare me for the journey to Sarphu. A journey into my own heart, and the heart of Kyimolung." I sit in meditation and feel simple love for my children, my husband, Yeshe and all my loved ones, and this love melts me a little more. My heart becomes soft, like honey. My trips to Nepal have meant leaving Mike and the kids for extended stretches of time. For many years now, my dreams have necessitated travelling halfway across the globe and into some of the most remote cracks and precipices on the planet. My dreams of Happy Valley have pulled me here. Yet I sense a change happening inside me. Being in this cave has fulfilled a dream, yet I don't feel the romantic potency I experienced when I first came here. At that time, I was moved to tears, my vision changed and internal earthquakes were set off when I looked at Milarepa. Now it's more like I'm having coffee with an old friend. I wonder: What will happen if I actually do make it to the epicentre of Happy Valley, and this love story reaches its finale? What happens when a recurring dream makes it final loop? Images of my family swell inside my mind, and I sense the coming death of something. But if I look very carefully, there is also a tiny new seed with the faintest glimmer of potential. The seed holds something for all four of us, something I don't quite know yet.

I'm onto the second butter lamp now, which I place on the hanger. I climb into my sleeping bag, then *poof*! It goes out. I'm left in a black so black that when I bulge my eyes open as wide as they can possibly go, I still see absolutely nothing. The dark feels both totally empty and outrageously full. My nervous system is primed. I feel the flicker of every silver moth wing, and my ears comb the silence for the sound of rodent claws on stone. Time expands almost grotesquely, and it takes an eternity to reach 8:45 p.m. Eventually, I realize I hear no rats, and my body softens, just slightly, and drifts into an almost conscious sleep. I awaken at 11 p.m., thinking it's morning, but I still have the whole night ahead of me. At some point my body uncoils at yet a deeper level, and I rest. At 5:30 a.m, a cool, clear light crawls through the window and door cracks and pulls me from sleep. I sync myself to nature's rhythms and wake with the sun.

Before leaving, I sweep out the cave. I clear all that needs to be cleared, both inside the cave and inside of me. I feel it now: I'm ready to pass through the Eastern Gate of Kyimolung.

Lamagaun, Tsum, September 17

I meet our porters at Tanzin's house. Rinzin and Tenzin will be carrying our heavy load of tents, stoves, food and supplies. I tease Tanzin that he should have found another Tenzin so all the guys could have the same name. Tenzin is 23 years old and in the prime of youth. His hair is tied into a high ponytail to reveal an undercut. He has the air of a young stallion – fiery, but also a little shy and in the learning process of life. Rinzin is around 40 and was in Sarphu five years ago, collecting wild garlic and yartsa gunbu (*Cordyceps sinensis*), a fungus called "summer grass" that sprouts from the little dead bodies of caterpillars, and is prized in Chinese medicine. Pickers comb the ground above 4000 metres, searching for this strange entity, as it currently fuels the new economy in this region. Rinzin made several perilous crossings from Sarphu to Tibet. We feel he will be a great addition of local knowledge to our team. He has chocolate eyes and a sinuous body from carry-ing heavy loads and living the mountain life.

When Ani Pema appears, we load our gear, wait out a heavy onslaught of rain, then heave the gear onto our backs, cover it with great sheets of plastic to stave off the wetness, and head down valley toward lower Tsum.

The monsoon doesn't want to quit, and by the time we reach our destination, a tiny village called Gho, we're soaked. We turn in at the village's only guest house. After changing out of our wet clothes, we head to the eating room, and spread maps and documents across a table. It's time to flesh out the details of "Expedition Sarphu." The main directions we will use come from the translated neyig[14] Yeshe sent me. It's a seven-page document that gives obscure directions like this: "Taking a stick you should go up near to the waterfall. After a short distance, the distance of an arrow shot, to the right, climb a doorstep; then you will have to climb the rock ladder." It seems part guidebook, part riddle. It describes how you should behave inside the beyul. There should be no fighting, no violence, no sex, and a deep respect for the land and people. It also gives detailed descriptions of the treasures Padmasambhava hid.

The place guide describes the shape of Kyimolung as a lotus flower, or female anatomy, depending on one's interpretation, and dictates that pilgrims must enter through one of the gates located at each of the four cardinal directions. Spiritual beings fiercely protect these gates, and if the timing isn't auspicious, or if one's karma isn't good, the protectors can unleash hail, snow and rock slides to prevent one from entering the secret land.

People who travel to the beyul for spiritual purposes view it as having the shape of a mandala, which is a symbolic image

---

14   Shared with me by Yeshe Palmo and Tenzing Lhundup. The original copy belongs to the Nile Labrang, entitled *Place Guide (neyik) for sKyid mo lung (Kymolung) – Valley of Happiness*. Copied from a terma revealed by Rigs 'dzin rGod Kyi Idem (Rigzin Godem).

representing layers of the mind and the cosmos. Yogis travel through the physical landscape in order to enter deeper mental states. By moving through outer consciousness, to inner, what's known as "secret," consciousness, or "Buddha mind," one can become enlightened. The physical act of moving through Happy Valley brings yogis back to their first nature. Tashi Palsang[15] serves as the ultimate goal; it holds the greatest number of Padmasambhava's treasures. We are just a 20-minute walk from the Eastern Gate now, and I'm humming with that beautiful feeling of being on the threshold of a great journey.

The guest house owner tells us that the nomads in Sarphu will be leaving imminently with their herds of dzo to avoid the coming snowfall, but we may get lucky and see them. The nomads may hold first-hand knowledge of Kyimolung's stories, and we hope they will point out some sacred sites.

We are so new to this journey, and there are many puzzle pieces to fit together.

Tanzin and I sketch out the secret valley in my coil notebook. Ani Pema and Rinzin discuss a special rock face in Sarphu that has self-arising images — sacred images that appear in nature — and they tell us about yak houses, the abandoned temple, and a self-arising stupa. We begin to populate our hand-drawn map with information. We are uncertain which side of the river we should hike up on. It seems most of the sacred sites are on the river's left side, yet Yeshe took the right-hand route in 1999. Twelve years ago, Ani Pema's group also went up the river's right side, and the right side is where the self-arising stupa is located. It seems the 2015 earthquakes caused massive damage, sheering off gargantuan swaths of mountain, and that the right-hand route is unmanageable. We consider the possibility of hiking up the left side, all the way to a massive glacier I'd seen on Google Earth, crossing the glacier, then exploring the right-hand side of the valley. That way we could visit the treasure locations while still attempting to visit

---

15   It is the highest peak in the Sringi Himal Range.

the stupa. Ani looks at us like we're crazy, saying there is no need to go to the stupa, and that we can simply look up at it and enjoy the view. She recommends we hike in and out on the left side.

Rinzin adds that the glacier we are thinking of crossing has made a massive retreat in recent years, and that lower down it has become a moving rock moraine and is very dangerous.

"We cannot cross the valley anymore," says Rinzin. "We used to walk over the ice to cross the river, but now it's water." This glacier I'd seen on Google Earth had an almost tidal pull on me. I knew I must see it, touch it, feel the immensity of its rock and ice – and now I wonder how much of it has disappeared.

We are really into it now, all of us sharing information spanning a timeline of more than a thousand years.

"Maybe we can try to make a bridge across the river," someone suggests.

"We could use the beams from a yak house, then return them when we are done," suggests someone else.

"Maybe we can go up much higher, toward the Tibet border, to find a way to cross," comes another suggestion. Our expedition begins to take form.

Through a guest house window we see an old temple and a few simple stone huts. Apparently, there is an old man in the village with information about Sarphu. Ani Pema disappears to try to find him, and when she returns she's full of stories. The old man spoke of memories and lore. There is a gate, he said, akin to a vagina. If it opens to the pilgrim, the pilgrim will see 108 houses inside. Some are wood, some stone, some clay. Also, if one puts a seed into the earth at night in Sarphu, the plant will be fully grown by morning, its yield ready to eat. The grandfather also sang a short song about the stupa. The translated lyrics state:

Great land of upper Sarphu valley
The natural stupa of crystal;
There is no way for circumambulation.
Make three prostrations and return.

"Everyone in Tsum knows this song," confirms Tanzin.

Grandfather also told her about a sacred rock called Senge Dongpa Chen, which is said to be protected by a fierce blue female Buddha who looks like a snow lion.[16]

Tanzin translates another interesting piece of information: "The old man says that there is a narrow passage next to the gompa, a tight opening in the rock. It's called Khandro Sanglam. If you can fit through the opening, it means you have good karma."

The group giggles, and Tanzin turns to me.

"Khandro Sanglam means vagina.[17] It translates as 'sacred way.'" I'm grateful Tanzin isn't afraid to clearly translate for my benefit. And I'm so excited, because, as I'd suspected, Kyimolung honours the power of the female.

"In Hinduism, they celebrate the lingam (Shiva temples have sacred penises inside). But in our culture, there are more sanglams (vaginas)." He grins. This is certainly true of Himalayan beyul. Ian Baker's book *The Heart of the World*, about Pemako beyul, another sacred valley far east of here, describes the entire sacred landscape as the form of the goddess Dorje Phagmo (in Sanskrit, Vajravarahi).

Outside the night has turned black, but we all want to meet this interesting old man. The stories are intriguing, many confirming information I'd brought from home. We creep out of the guest house and follow narrow beams of light emitted by our phones to a cold, stone, one-room house. Inside, sitting upon a bed, is a smiling Elder named Tenzin Palsang. He has big floppy ears, and

---

16 Senge Dongpa Chen is the *secret aspect* of Guru Rinpoche. This refers to the inner guru, or the non-dual teacher. In Vajrayana Buddhism, there are human teachers with human faults and attributes. There are also representations of emptiness, the ultimate teacher, which is beyond human form. Senge Dongpa Chen, also called Senge Dongma Chen, represents an enlightened aspect of Guru Rinpoche/Padmasambhava; the inner form beneath his outer human form.

17 Tenzing Lhundup, Nile Labrang, gives a further translation of Khandro Sanglam: kha = sky; dro = goer; sang = secret; lam = path, way, passage, etc. Secret path can be understood in the vast teachings of Vajrayana Buddhism, and also as a vagina.

his nose is smudged with charcoal. He wears a skullcap, and a wooden rosary dangles from his neck.

His wife ushers us in. She barely reaches my shoulder in height. The grandparents' hut has no insulation, and the bed is pushed up to the bare, stacked stones. Their possessions might fit in a single bag. They are beaming.

Tanzin sidles up beside Grandfather and gives him a bottle of whisky as an offering. Grandfather is hard of hearing, so Tanzin cups his hands around his right ear and yells in our questions one by one.

I sit on the bed next to Grandfather, and he puts an arm around me as we pose for a photo. We are all laughing – almost giddy. Somehow sharing this information is a super-happy event. The joy spreads like fire glow from this warm nest out into the inky night.

The Eastern Gate of Kyimolung, September 18

> The door is a narrow one, and has an inaccessible gorge. When [one gets] through this, the area becomes spacious. There are nutritious grains here; and whatever grains you plant will grow. Even the plants that don't normally grow will also grow naturally. There are various kinds of herbs. Inside this place, in the higher and lower reaches, the nomads and farmers will live.[18]
>
> —Translated from the Nile Labrang's neyig

We depart from Gho and hike to a steel suspension bridge slung across the silver Sarphu River. This is our entrance, and the place guide says, "East there is a door of water and rock," and names the village of Retsam (known on present-day maps as Renjam). We have arrived at the Eastern Gate. From here, everything I see will be new. The valley walls rise high, and are clothed in uncountable shades of green. You can spot this bridge from Google Earth, but

---

18 *Place Guide (neyik) for sKyid mo lung (Kymolung) – Valley of Happiness* (translation commissioned by Yeshe Palmo, 2001), 2.

trying to virtually navigate the Sarphu Valley we are about to enter requires skill, because if your finger slips a little on the track pad, you'll get lost inside a mountain. There is little navigable space – virtually or literally. We are about to squeeze through an earthly portal into a wild and different world.

Taking local advice, we cross the bridge to the river's left side and enter the inner sanctum. The beginning of the trail is good and has had use. Our group of five begins walking through a verdant jungle of bamboo and massive rhododendron trees, whose pinkish bark gleams in the wet. I see familiar plants like columbine and wild rhubarb, as well as many unfamiliar flowers. Sometimes the earth we pad is black, other times, russet. Our boots squish into it, and somehow, even in this muck, Tanzin's pants remain clean.

Ani Pema has found herself a handsome bamboo walking stick with smooth, strong bark.

We pass a yak house, then a second by mid-morning. The second yak house appears to be empty. We shed our heavy loads and rest upon some unseen nomad's field. Aggressive nettle bushes erupt from the soil, looking fierce with their hairy, warty, stinging (yet delicious) leaves. Seemingly out of nowhere, a young boy arrives carrying a blackened kettle. Tanzin pulls out steel cups from our load, and soon we're having our morning coffee. This would never happen in Alberta, I think, and I smile as the caffeine works its way into my veins.

Ahead is the place on Google Earth that looks impenetrable. A massive, phallic erection of rock rises from the valley bottom, and somehow we must get around it.

"Look, Jane. We will go up there, beyond that ridge," says Tanzin. I get my first taste of how much endurance I will need for our expedition. I look at Tanzin and align my eyes with where his finger is pointing. It's aimed at a place where a slightly horizontal blip in a ridge will allow us to climb beyond. I take a picture and put an arrow on it, then show Tanzin to be sure I've understood correctly.

"Yes, that ridge." I nod, swallow deeply, and a huge ascent begins. We slide through the mud, and Ani Pema hikes up her robe so it won't get soiled. The ascent is arduous, and the jungle envelops us with emerald arms. We become completely soaked.

We ascend from 2430 metres to 3630 metres, and the vegetation shrinks, becoming bushes and herbs. We break away from the gorge toward a massively overhung cliff. It forms a rain shadow, and is being used by a father and his son, a boy of perhaps 10 years, who sit together watching the rain and waterfalls. The father's fingers are at work as he weaves a halter for one of their dzo. They look perfectly content, though surprised to see our group. The son plays peek-a-boo with us, hiding from our hellos and smiles. We make the decision to camp here to avoid setting up our tents in the mud. Soon we are clicking together tent poles and inflating sleeping mats. Ani Pema and I will sleep in a green tent, and Tanzin, Tenzin and Rinzin in a slightly larger orange tent.

The nomad confirms that another expedition came through some months before – Phunjo's group, whom we'd heard about back at the clinic. He tells us they were in the valley for about four days, then he offers us firewood. We squish ourselves under the cliff's shadow, and soon a fire is glowing. We pull off boots and peel away wet socks to dry them out as best we can, then sacrifice my stainless steel cooking pot to the fire. It is filled with water, balanced on well-placed rocks, and put directly over the flames. "This will save our fuel," says Tanzin. It's more authentic too, I think, as my pot blackens with carbon. Ani Pema rifles through our North Face duffle bag and chooses a freeze-dried meal called "Korean Hot and Spicy Chicken." After soaking the contents with hot water, she gives it a try. Her lips turn red, and I watch as her face registers distinct dislike.

"Is it okay, Ani? It looks like you don't like it." She gives a half-smile, eats one more bite, then walks to the bushes and dumps out the rest in a great big slosh. She wipes her lips, which actually look swollen from the spice. When we read the label, we find a description stating that pregnant women, old people and people with heart conditions should avoid eating this meal.

The Tsumpas laugh and joke a lot. I can tell they're teasing each other and cracking jokes. It is not a shy culture, and there is much

Julie and Mike in Morocco.

Ben in Ait Bougemez.

Our guide, Ahmad, showing our family his homeland in Ait Bougemez.

Family homestay and dinner in Ait Bougemez.

(*right*) Ben, Jane and Julie enjoy breakfast at a homestay in Ait Bougemez.

(*bottom*) A high view of Ait Bougemez, above Ahmad's family's guest house.

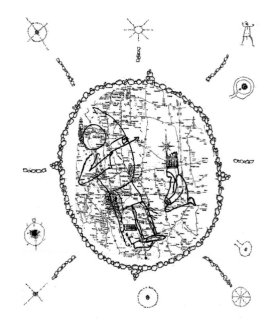

Nāāpi and the Old Woman. Map drawn by Stan Knowlton, head interpreter at Head-Smashed-In Buffalo Jump/Pissk'ān, as experienced in his Vision Quests.

Courtesy Stan Knowlton.

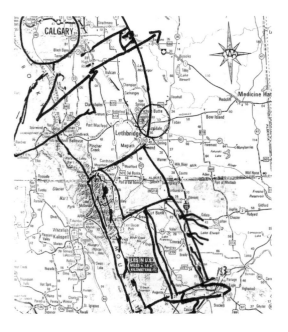

Nāāpi and the Land. Map drawn by Stan Knowlton, Head Interpreter at Head-Smashed-In Buffalo Jump/Pissk'ān. As experienced in his Vision Quests.

Courtesy of Stan Knowlton.

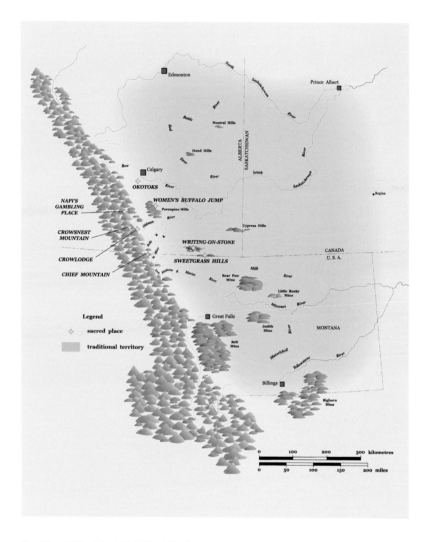

Traditional Blackfoot/Soki-Tapi Territory. Courtesy the Glenbow Museum.

Grandma Joyce on her road trip. Stopping for a beer in Lundbreck, Alberta.

Conrad Little Leaf/Piita Piikoan at Head-Smashed-In Buffalo Jump/Pissk'ān.

View of the Oldman River/Nââpi-iítahtaa, near where we spread Grandpa Jim's ashes.

Jane on Nââpi's spine.

Ken Williams on Nââpi's spine, looking back toward "The Gap."

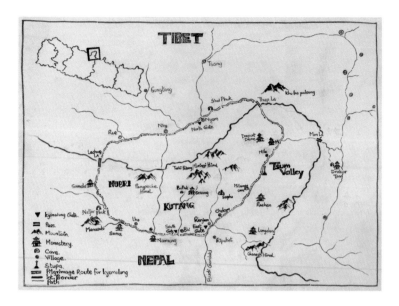

Map of Kyimolung beyul, based on Yeshe Palmo's drawings from her 1999 expedition. Illustration courtesy Sangay Phuntsok.

Map of Sarphu Valley, Tsum, based on Jane's expedition. Some of the place names were shared by nomad Tsewang Norbu, and others come from the neyig. Illustration courtesy Sangay Phuntsok.

(*right*) Ani Pema making noodles at Drephuet Dronme Nunnery, Tsum.

(*bottom*) Ani Pema and Jane Marshall in Tsum.

Lama Sherap Tendar Rinpoche, head of the Nile Labrang, Tsum.

Students, parents, Tanzin (left) and Ward Chief Lama Pasang (centre, in red) gathering for a school photo in Lamagaun, Tsum.

Ani Pema, Tanzin, Tenzin and Rinzin drying out shoes at Camp 1, Sarphu.

Looking back at our trail
from the high point before
Camp 2, Sarphu.

This yak hut at Camp 2
became our cook tent.
We were grateful for a dry
place to spend time.

Camp 2, Sarphu.
Views of Ganesh Himal
bordering Tibet.

Ani Pema looking up valley to the Sarphu River.

Ani Pema at the crumbling Sarphu Gompa, built by the first Drukpa Rinpoche.

Ani Pema and I climb to
Senge Dongpa Chen,
the rock at skyline.

The north end of the ridge near Senge Dongpa
Chen. Lingering in the sunset, with the glacier
below.

Tenzin and I navigate the many ridges that line the way to Tashi Palsang.

Looking up the glacier to Tashi Palsang, where the greatest number of treasures are held.

Team Sarphu! Ani Pema, Jane, Tenzin, Rinzin and Tanzin at Tashi Palsang.

Our wild camp spot on the spur. You can see our orange tent, with the glacier to the left.

A blue poppy that the Tsumpas were interested in.

Serang Monastery, on the other side of Tashi Palsang in the Nubri region.

Larkye Pass on the Manaslu Circuit.

Jane with the 17th Drakar Rinpoche at his home in Swayambhu.

A final goodbye to Drakar Rinpoche as he snaps a photo and we ride off on Tanzin's bike. Photo courtesy Drakar Rinpoche.

humour. Ani Pema is still quiet with me around the boys and not comfortable speaking English, so I resign myself to being the minority. This allows me to watch faces and body language and re-engage with the few Tibetan words I know. Yet as soon as we wriggle into our tent Ani Pema and I tell stories and begin to have laughing attacks. Our situation is pretty ridiculous, really. We've left all comfort behind to shiver in wet clothes and sleep on the ground. Quite the predicament, yet it feels right. She shows me photos and videos on her iPhone, we make a few more jokes, then we fall asleep to the sound of waterfalls as they dive off the mountains.

The Hike to Camp 2, September 19

> Pilgrimage always involves a journey with risk. In accepting that risk, whether it is through penance, devotion or hard travel, pilgrims find the renewal they seek.
>
> —KATRINA ROSEN, *With You By Bike*

I'm pulled from sleep by the sound of water. It forms different sounds: a tinkle on the plastic that protects the Tsumpas' packs, a gush from the waterfalls and streams that rolls over and off the mountains, and the subtle sound of the clouds becoming rain-laden, then releasing. We begin a stiff ascent to a pass above the cliff, and then the craziness really begins. Imagine a long row of mountains with peaks rising to over 7000 metres. The uppermost grooves and troughs hold mythic, glacial ice. These glaciers thin, then melt into numerous waterfalls that glide down the stony alpine into a world of green jungle and the Sarphu River below. The starting elevation of Sarphu Valley is approximately 2400 meters, and the highest point of the Sringi Range is over 7000 meters. That's more than four and a half vertical kilometres! This is storybook landscape, too big and bold for the regular mind to fathom. If you look at the topographic lines on a map, it's like an artist got overzealous with their line drawing, creating tight terrace steps ascending to heaven. Our job now is to follow a thin but existent nomad path etched across the flanks of these glorious mountains. A huge traverse begins.

We come to a fast-flowing stream. The route seems impossible, blocked by a cliff. Yet some industrious path maker has reinforced the cliff with strategic rocks that form a couple of steps in the rock face. Rinzin takes the lead. His big load – held by a supportive forehead strap – doesn't deter him. He finds natural, small footholds, walks across the reinforced section and makes his way across unscathed. I'm not so sure. In my early twenties, I spent a lot of time sport climbing and bouldering, and I realize I now need to employ those skills. A slip will mean a five-metre fall into a stream bed.

"Well, the exposure isn't so bad. At least it's not a huge drop below," I say to Tanzin, assessing the route.

"Yes, but falling here would cause serious injury. Be careful."

Our other porter Tenzin takes my pack and shows me the way. My hands grip the stone, and it feels wet but solid. The Tsumpas know the dependability of the rock by its colour and texture, and they show me how to avoid the slippery black sections. Sure enough, there are enough positive holds to cling to with confidence.

"Easy!" declares 23-year-old Tenzin after we make it across. I release a deep breath. *Easy*.

Ridge after ridge, waterfall after waterfall, we make a grand ascending traverse. With the high level of difficulty, our group begins to synchronize out of basic need. We begin to hold hands on exposed sections, and reach up to support someone's boot, creating a human foothold when the stone lacks the necessary features. The nervousness of being in a new group begins to fade as we return to our primal natures in Happy Valley.

"Your past has helped you," observes Tanzin as we use various climbing moves to stretch and reach our hands to grasp for rock and grip the stalks of strong plants. He's referring to climbing and yoga (I'm a yoga teacher, and have practised for 17 years). I reflect on this as we ascend. Many things had to mature for this journey to happen. My body needed to be strong; at 38, my form carries within it critical muscle memory. The muscles themselves know just what to do – how to slightly adjust to ensure stability, how to pivot, bend, flex and reach – from dangling off stalactites in Thailand, to navigating the backcountry of Alberta, to my past trips to Tsum's unique landscape. My mind also needed to mature as I studied beyul information and made other trips to Nepal. I needed the texture and lore of Kyimolung beyul to grow inside of me. I needed the people to share their stories with me. I feel that this trip couldn't have happened a day sooner. It's a trip that needed to ripen naturally, and I had to be ready for it too. Not only do I carry the weight of my pack, I also bear the weighted responsibility of writing about a sacred land.

Tanzin plucks a wild rhubarb stalk and nibbles on the stringy, red fruit. He calls them *pangju*. Their rubbery leaves fan out to 2 metres across and are beginning to blush red from the changing season. They decorate the mountain flanks and form ornaments against the green. The fertile land all around is herbal. Slowly, my nose begins to recognize different scents I've never smelled before. Our journey will be subtly perfumed by nature. Often, Ani Pema plucks herbs and tucks them into her pocket. Many are used traditionally in incense and Tibetan medicine. At special places, she pulls out incense sticks and adds the herbs, making offerings to appease the mountain spirits and the Buddhas as it says to do in Padmasambhava's guidebook. Now we are in a land where deities and spirits inhabit the mountains, and where the energy of fully enlightened Buddhas glows bright. They all must be recognized, honoured and appeased.

The trail leads us to a pass at 4465 metres. Prayer flags flutter between a stone *chorten* (similar to a stupa – a sacred structure) and the mountainside. The cloud lifts just enough to show us the full route we've hiked, and to be perfectly honest, it seems impossible that our bodies found enough horizontal purchase to accomplish the traverse. There are at least nine stream crossings, and the angles scramble my mind. Our high elevation has lifted us to the snow line, and water crystallizes around us in lacy, white patterns. We can see way back to our starting point, to where Tsum Valley and Sarphu Valley merge.

We can now see far up the valley too. Rinzin and Ani Pema are excited, and break into a whirlwind of Tibetan as their memories of this place are reignited. Ani Pema gazes across the valley to the old nomad route that is no longer used. A huge slab of the mountain has cracked off, making the old route mostly obsolete.

Looking up valley, Rinzin describes his previous route to Tibet, which crossed even more ridges, then made a left-hand turn to the glacier before continuing north over the international border.

Cloud returns to smother out our views, and shivers creep across our damp bodies. We descend to 4310 metres and find an empty yak house, its front door sealed by a stone slab. Before I can blink, the porters have heaved it aside, entered and lit a fire. We begin the daily process of cramming together and holding our various socks, insoles and dirty boots to dry over a bath of smoke. Rinzin and Ani Pema take some of our cooking oil and begin rubbing it into their feet and calf muscles, giving themselves a foot massage in the warmth of the fire.

Inside, it is small and simple: stacked firewood on the hearth wall, a few shelves built into the stone, and even a little altar, holding no deities but rather delicate wildflowers cradled in a plastic pop bottle. The dirt floor is nearly frozen, and a tarp has been pulled across the stones to form the roof. We populate the hut with our assortment of gear and feel incredibly grateful to be cooking inside rather than out in the rain.

Later, the evening sky clears to reveal just how spectacularly we're situated. Vanguard mountains form protective walls on both sides of the valley. North, the valley collides with a peak and is forced to change course and turn westward. My satellite device shows that beyond the left-hand turn is the alluring glacier I'd seen on Google Earth. The glacier forms the pathway to Tashi Palsang, the mysterious mountain I ache to discover. Even from here, I feel her pull, but for now she remains hidden.

Across the valley and high up one of the mountains, we spot a cave with a large rock protrusion in front. This is the crystal stupa the Elder in Gho told us about. Ani Pema saw it 12 years ago and is fascinated by it once again. Back in Lamagaun, when we were leaving, she'd insisted that the head lama/village Chief, Lama Pasang, go and fetch his binoculars so we could bring them along with us. She had no shyness about his status, or about waiting while he rummaged through his house to find them. She uses them now, and swears she can see crystals growing out the top of the stupa. The cave behind it looks massive, and I voice a wish to perhaps find a way to climb up to it – even though the local song says there is no way to circumambulate it, and that you should simply prostrate three times and return. The guidebook describes it in detail, saying, "In the middle of this place is a self-arising chorten, like the top of a tent, and there are seven supreme major treasures there and another seven terma [the treasures hidden in the 8th century by the yogi Padmasambhava] of immediate need, which have enough long life water to satisfy seven thirsty men."[19] Eric Fabry told me the cave is impossible to reach these days, unless one can fly, since directly below is where the mountain cracked off during the 2015 earthquake, leaving a smooth, sheer wall.

The sun sets, and Ani Pema and I press through the half-frozen mud to our tent situated below the yak house. We hang our socks and undies from various inner loopholes, knowing they will never dry, look at each other, and again burst out laughing at this style of living. She lifts her robes to show me her thighs. They are littered with little red bumps.

"So itchy!" she proclaims, as I advise her to not scratch. Young Tenzin has the same problem. Earlier he'd pulled up his shirt to reveal his entire back covered in bites. Tanzin carefully dabbed hydrocortisone cream from his first aid kit onto each of the hundreds of red marks on his friend's back. I have a few on my arms and suspect they are flea bites.

---

19 *Place Guide (neyik) for sKyid mo lung (Kymolung) – Valley of Happiness* (translation commissioned by Yeshe Palmo, 2001), 3.

Ani Pema and I are real sisters now, changing together, living together, going to the bathroom together (which means guarding the area while taking turns squatting), and examining each other's ailments. As I rest in the cozy down of my sleeping bag, body on the earth, I look over at my friend. Though she's a celibate nun removed from the ordinary world, she's in this world as much as (or more than) anyone. She laughs loud, teases, and everyone wants to talk with her. Being a nun like Ani Pema is about living with raucous joy.

Tonight our team sleeps in the inner chambers near the heart of the valley of happiness. And, indeed, I am happy.

The Heart of the Beyul

Inside the Treasure Map, September 20

This Hidden Valley of Happiness is blessed especially by a wealth of spiritual treasures known as *terma*. For the benefit of future generations, Guru Padmasambhava prepared spiritual treasures in the form of texts and sacred objects, and had them hidden in various places in Tibet, Nepal, and Bhutan. A variety of these...have been revealed...in the mountain of Sringi Himal [Tashi Palsang].[20]

—SERANG MONASTERY, *Bunch of Lotus*

---

20 The Serang Monastery magazine lists Kyimolung's treasures, revealed by tertön Garwang Dorge (1640–1685), as: 1) the Mirror of the Enlightened Mind of Vajrasattva; 2) the Great Compassionate One, the Heart Essence of the Three Roots; 3) the Unsurpassed Innermost Oral Lineage of Padmasambhava; 4) the Self-Illuminating Dharmadhatu: The Profound Essence; 5) Burning Cutting Blade of Vajrakilaya; and 6) Cutting through Afflicted Emotions (Chöd). *Bunch of Lotus: A Commemorative Brochure*, Sangchen Rabten Norbu Ling Foundation, November 2017, 77.

The night was again filled with rain chatter, the fluid voice of inclement weather speaking from the heavens into the curve of the valley. But now it is morning, and it is quiet. I unzip the tent fly with hope in my belly. The view almost knocks me back into my tent – the scene before me is potent. Clear, almost crystalline, and full of wet sparkles. The sky is a spacey, early-morning blue, not yet fully lit by the sun, and the day holds so much potential. Ani Pema peers at me from her sleeping bag.

"Good weather!" I yell, then reach in and hug her.

I have awoken inside the treasure map that has captivated me for years. Now I am adding my own gentle footsteps to spiritual history. My heart throbs with the immediacy of being right here, right now.

We look down toward the Sarphu River, our eyes angled up valley, and can now see the abandoned gompa. It looks to be in bad repair, and the roof has fallen in.

Looking up, on our side of the river, we see a high pass dusted with snow. In its saddle a large rock outcrop pokes up to breach the blue. The place guide says this rock belongs to a fully enlightened female Buddha named Senge Dongpa Chen. If you look at a symbolic image of her, she is cobalt blue, bare-breasted and has the face of a fierce snow lion. She dances wildly, with a body of coiled power. Under one foot, she crushes human corpses, while the other knee flares out, her heel drawn in close to her groin in ecstasy. She holds a spear of severed heads, and wears a necklace of them too. Her mane flares; fangs are bared, eyes are bulbous. She stands on a lotus flower with voluptuous lip-like petals. Senge Dongpa Chen cuts through delusion, confusion, misunderstanding and (at least for me) unnecessary religious baggage. She is the secret, innermost aspect of Padmasambhava in the tantric belief system. We have come to the place where this strong energy presides. If this is Senge Dongpa Chen's power, let it be mine too, I think. Let me travel as Jane, light yet grounded, fiery and fierce if I need to be, naked and open, so I can tell the story of Kyimolung in a way that's as crisp and pure as this glistening morning. For this Happy Valley story goes deeper than gender, hierarchy and religion. It represents the deepest core of being human. We are in primal land, untouched by human convention. This land is unsanitized, and the mountains rule. The mighty Himalayas wear their elemental adornments of snow, water, stone and flowers. The place guide enlivens everything we see with a mythic layer of multigenerational perspective. When I see a rock, it is a rock, but now it's also home to Senge Dongpa Chen. The ancient words stored carefully in my backpack become our world and the key to deeply understanding this place.

We have become children in an adventure story, ready to explore.

After breakfast, we split into two groups: Tanzin and Tenzin will attempt to cross the valley in order to scout a possible route to the crystal, self-arising stupa. First, the guys will have to climb up valley, cross the glacier and get to the other side, though we fear the glacier at this point is actually a deep river. Looking down, the valley walls have been fissured by earthquakes and pulled apart by the retreating glacier. The lower regions of the mountains below us are in a chaotic state of loose dirt and rock tenuously balanced at sharp angles. Looking toward the stupa, there's the vertical stone wall, then a bit of intriguing green grass, another cliff band, and finally the cave and prominent rock. A waterfall slides down the right-hand side of their proposed ascent line. The entire route has massive exposure, meaning that a fall without rope at certain critical points would be fatal. It looks impossible, but so did the route we already came from. We've brought a rope and harnesses for a case like this, so the guys load up the gear and set off.

Ani Pema, Rinzin and I will descend to the ruined gompa. We hope to find the area's single nomad, rumoured to be a local lama, who may have information to share. The place guide instructs us to trust the local people and ask them for help, saying, "Border people and wild beasts protect the Buddha's words and they are messengers."[21] I consider the value of local knowledge. In my

---

21 *Place Guide (neyik) for sKyid mo lung (Kymolung) – Valley of Happiness* (translation commissioned by Yeshe Palmo, 2001), 3.

avalanche training back in Canada, local knowledge of the terrain and snow conditions was really important. Here, too, we must rely on local wisdom, such as what we received from Tenzin Palsang, the old man of Gho in the little rock hut.

I've brought a coil notebook with me and have written down key questions I have for the nomad, wishing to confirm what I've read in the various texts and academic papers on Kyimolung. I've scribbled down in pencil:

1. Where is Tashi Palsang?
2. Where is Senge Dongpa Chen (the lion-faced rock)?
3. Where are the self-arising images?
4. In the texts, they say there is a rock circled by many caves that has lots of treasure. Where is this?
5. Where is the treasure (terma) that is the body of the princess – daughter of the Tibetan King Trisong Detsen?

I tuck my notebook into my pack, and we begin a gentle descent. The sun actually has heat today; it warms us and highlights the wild strawberry runners knitted across the slope.

The gompa sits near the edge of a gently inclining bench. To the right, a long, decisive line marks the end of the green, and then the view tumbles off a cataclysmic drop to the Sarphu River.

The gompa was built by the first Drukpa Rinpoche Sherap Dorje (1872–1945), one of the lama guardians of Tsum, also known as *Labrang*. He is a famous lama in Tsum's history, and is revered for his vision even today. A century ago, he and the previous incarnation of my teacher[22] declared Tsum a zone of nonviolence. Villagers signed a document with their fingerprints, promising they wouldn't hunt or slaughter animals in Tsum because of its beyul status. The local people continue to renew this pact, and thus this region is brimming with protected flora and fauna. I'm

---

22   The 16 Tulku of Drakar Taso tulku Tenzin Norbu, recognized by the 16th Karmapa.

in a zone that's home to more than 33 species of mammals (like snow leopards, musk deer and blue sheep), 2,000 species of plants, 11 types of forests, 3 species of reptiles, 60 types of medicinal plants, 110 species of birds and 11 species of butterflies.[23] The mountains hum with life. The land is springy and verdant, and everything is sheltered – free of biting winds because of the valley's extreme depth. We are protected by the geography of this hidden land.

Everything glows in the scene before us. It's as if it's been painted with strokes of yellow sunshine.

We approach the temple. Time has added gold and black lichen and soft emerald moss to the fallen stones. We each take a kata and circumambulate the front chorten, then walk through an open door. The roof is almost entirely collapsed, so we awkwardly climb over fallen slate shingles. The sky above is bright and pours its radiance into the ruined temple.

We find a central pillar still standing and take turns tying katas around it. Ani Pema and Rinzin light incense, and then Ani Pema offers prayers, her voice bringing a warm human touch.

A dog's bark cracks the calm, and its volume climbs as we hear it run closer. Guard dogs in Tsum villages are super scary. They are a hybrid breed of Tibetan mastiff, with big, ferocious teeth. I stay hidden behind a latticed window. A nomad appears and calls back his dog, which is actually a friendly puppy. Rinzin reaches out his hands and ruffles the dog's fur, and they become fast friends.

We emerge and walk with the nomad to the edge of the embankment, where earth surrenders to river. The nomad's name is Tsewang Norbu, and he is the only person in the upper valley. Half of his chin-length hair is tied up. Red rubber boots protect his feet, and he wears an army jacket mottled with camouflage.

---

23   See Nima Lama and Jailab Kumar Rai, "Tsum Sacred Conservation Area in Gorkha, Nepal," 2013, http://www.env.go.jp/en/nature/asia-parks/pdf/wg3/APC_WG3-23_Nima%20Lama%20and%20Jailab%20Kumar%20Rai.pdf.

His manner seems gentle and slow. Tsewang is the son of the lama we'd heard about, and luckily he has learned from his father about the beyul lore. Rinzin lies down on his belly to peer over the edge into the abyss, while the puppy gnaws on his shoe. Soon we are all belly down on the ground, as our heads reach over the cliff to gaze at an unfathomable drop.

Ani Pema asks Tsewang my Kyimolung questions. He tells us that Tashi Palsang is indeed the same as Sringi Himal, the name recognized by Nepal. He also tells us it is known locally as Zhonglha Karpo, meaning "a white place where someone stays," or "white god of the province." My blood runs fast when Tsewang mentions Tashi Palsang. We still can't see it from our current position. We will need to hike further. Tsewang also confirms that the lion rock, Senge Dongpa Chen, is indeed the outcrop above our camp, and that we can find self-arising images in the cliffs above the gompa. Then he invites us for tea at his yak hut, and offers to take us to a place called Ter Phuk, meaning "treasure cave."

This is the last yak house in the valley. It has been built into a boulder, and Tsewang has stretched a white tarp from the boulder to meet a low stone wall. He offers us seats inside, then goes to fetch water for tea. It gives me time to really look around. Midday sun is creating a greenhouse effect inside, and I open myself to the warmth. I'm so curious to see how Tsewang lives. He's been here almost four months in near isolation while living off the land and with the animals. A series of wooden buckets, hand-hewn from tree trunks, are stacked inside. There are also blue plastic containers caked with grime. A woven bamboo basket used for collecting animal fodder and firewood (Tibetan: *tselbo*) sits at rest near his hearth. The dwelling has an earthen floor and an altar.

Tsewang returns with a blackened kettle. He uses a small silver dagger called a *kukri*, splits a resinous wood chip for fire starter, and gets a blaze going. The Tsumpas' fire-making skills amaze me. They are so efficient, gentle and precise. Soon water rolls inside the kettle. He reaches for a cake of Tibetan tea, breaks off a piece, and it diffuses its flavour into the bubbling water. He then

lifts a tarp to reveal a massive lump of butter. It is creamy in colour, and looks rich and fatty. I get nervous and ask if I can stick
to plain black tea, without the butter. Normally I quite like this
drink, which is akin to salty soup, but I decide to be extra careful
with my health in this remote spot. Backcountry diarrhea is not
something I want to be a part of. He kindly pours the clear brew
into a tin cup for me. For Ani Pema and Rinzin, he reaches for
his tea churn (Tibetan: *dongmo*), and inside it he mixes the black
tea, butter and some salt for traditional butter tea. He churns and
churns and churns, then pours. Next he lifts the lid off a contain-
er and spoons clumps of white, unrefrigerated yogurt into bowls,
then adds roasted barley flour (Tibetan: *tsampa*).

"You try?" Ani Pema asks me. I tell her I'd better not. I doubt
my Western stomach could handle it under any circumstances.
She and Rinzin devour it, loving the local taste more than Korean
freeze-dried food, and they literally lick their bowls clean with
hungry, pink tongues.

Inside Tsewang's hut, I'm faced with a visceral feeling. I'm a
little queazy looking at his food, and I feel an intimacy being in
the place where he eats, sleeps and lives. I smell the earth and
animal dung and woodsmoke, and feel the heat radiating from
our own bodies, and it feels...uncensored. This is a life filled
with survival skills and practicalities, painted bright by the
surrounding elements. It is direct and unapologetic. Death and
mortality feel unnervingly close, yet in knowing this, life feels
magnified. Outside we hear calves crooning in a small stone
enclosure, while nearby their mother nuzzles the hillside plants.
They are Tsewang's lifeline and sustenance, as he spends months
pulling their milk and making dairy products.

When finished, Tsewang leads us outside to where he has spread
out large tarps covered with skinny tubes of something white.

"Yak cheese," says Ani Pema. It is laid out in the sun and air to
harden. Tsewang gathers a great bag full and offers it to us as a gift.

The bench we pad is riddled with unique boulders and caves,
and it reminds me of the place in Alberta where we spread my

grandfather's ashes, and the boulders on Naapi's spine. That was Grandpa's Happy Valley, and now I am in mine.

There is a shift in the weather; the valley breathes up cloud from below, and the sun submits to the density of cloud. Tsewang shows us the treasure cave.[24] The place guide states, "There is a rock in the middle which is circled by caves. There is a lot of terma hidden here."[25] The area is small, more of an overhang than a cave. Ani Pema and I climb inside. She makes incense offerings and opens her voice in prayer. It is amazing to imagine that a yogi once came here with a vision and pulled out texts from solid stone.

We walk again to the edge of the benchland, where the meadow gives way to landslide. Tsewang points out a path that breaches this thin line and tells us it will take us to the river below. It's possible that this could be a route to the self-arising crystal stupa that Tanzin and Tenzin are now scouting – a much shorter, more direct route. Rinzin looks over the brink and thinks it's possible for us to try, but Ani Pema and I share a concerned look. The drop makes our heads spin, and the earth appears fickle, ready to give way. It's a geographical threshold neither of us wants to cross.

Instead, we walk further up the bench and come to a larger cave called Khandro Sanglam.[26] This is what the old man told us

---

24 Lama Pema Gyamtso of Serang told me that terma was pulled from this Ter Phuk, and that it was one of two possible treasure teachings entitled Pema Nyengyud, or Dorsem Thuk Kyi Melong. Khenpo Tenzing Lhundup confirmed that different chapters of Pema Nyengyud were discovered at the tortoise rock (as stated in the tertön Tenzin Repa's biography). Additional treasure was also revealed nearby at a "brown standing rock," and from a "double triangle" rock. These texts were originally revealed by tertön Rigzin Godem, then hidden again at Senge Dongpa Chen, then rediscovered by tertön Garwang Dorje. The Pema Nyengyud text states that Guru Rinpoche hid the treasure himself. Lama Pema Gyamtso of Serang Monastery confirmed that tertön Garwang Dorje pulled treasure from this cave.

25 Place Guide (neyik) for sKyid mo lung (Kymolung) – Valley of Happiness (translation commissioned by Yeshe Palmo, 2001), 1.

26 Tibetan: Khandro. Sanskrit: Dakini. Meaning "sky dancer," or "sky goer." Sanglam means "sacred way," or "vagina."

about – the vagina/sacred way of the Khandro. Khandro translates as "sky dancer," or "sky goer," and represents the divine female principal of awakened energy. "On a secret level, [a khandro] is seen as the manifestation of fundamental aspects of phenomena and the mind, and so her power is intimately associated with the most profound insights of Vajrayana meditation," says the website Dakini Power, which features the foremost female Tibetan Buddhist teachers of our time. "In this her most essential aspect, she is called the formless wisdom nature of the mind itself."[27] If we make it through the sacred way, we will be born into this wisdom nature, into what is called Buddhahood, where one realizes that all things are ultimately empty of permanent form, yet shining with possibility and love.

There are two entrances: a larger one, and then a very tight portal. Ani Pema is laughing like a teenager in sex ed class. The men and I enter the cave and walk to the back, where we see the crack (that definitely looks like a vagina). Ani Pema is outside and will be the first to enter. She's quite a bit higher than us, and of course comes in headfirst. We watch as she wriggles in. This is no sanctified religious affair. She's laughing so hard she can hardly move. Finally, her feet come through, and she gathers herself on the cave floor. I go outside and do the same. As I squeeze through the portal, blood rushes to my head. It's a bit like a slow-motion, vaginal waterslide I'm taking headfirst. I enter the dark. But after all that struggle, we realize we've gone the wrong direction. We've literally gone from the outside world back into the womb!

This time, Ani Pema, Rinzin and I all climb out in the right direction. When Ani Pema reaches the outside world, she wails, "Wah, wah!" like a newborn baby. It seems our karma is at least good enough to get through, even after having made our initial mistake. Perhaps we first needed to crawl back inside the void before we were ready to reverse our course and face this uncertain

---

27   "Dakini (Sanskrit): A Female Messenger of Wisdom," Dakini Power, http://www.dakinipower.com/what-is-a-dakini.

world. We've been double blessed. Isn't this the spiritual path for many of us? First, we long to attain heaven or lasting peace, to leave this world of discomfort and uncertainty behind, to be in the womb where we have no responsibility. Where everything is perfect. But perhaps we ultimately realize there's no such thing as permanent heaven. If we can learn to live in Happy Valley, with its ups and downs, its discomfort, its vulnerable beauty, and be truly okay with that broad spectrum, only then are we totally free.

We re-enter the cave, and the mood stills and calms. Ani Pema investigates the sanglam more closely. The stone around the passageway has thin, milky ribs that look like grooves of muscle. She touches one and notes that it is wet. She blushes pink, then flicks the water three times on our foreheads as a blessing.

"Maybe tulku is here," she jokes. In Tibetan lore, if a realized being or master enters a dry cave, it can begin to drip. Perhaps it's Ani Pema herself who holds this power. There are stories that this happened to my friend, the 17th Drakar Rinpoche. When he was young, he left monastic life. It is said that Tsum people lost faith in him and didn't approve of his unorthodox lifestyle. Years later, he made a trip to the western part of Kyimolung. People saw auspicious symbols in the lakes and ponds and water where he'd passed. Water dripped from caves when he entered, they said, and their belief in him returned.

Ani Pema makes offerings on behalf of us all and places them on a small altar. I add my own offerings too. Before leaving for Nepal, I had asked Ken Williams if he could gather traditional Indigenous offerings from Blackfoot territory. Ken fosters two teenaged boys from the Piikani Nation, and the three of them had put together sacred items for this journey that include sage, a braid of sweetgrass, sweet pine needles, organic tobacco, a chip from a Sundance tree and a smidgen of bear root used for healing, and then they tied the bits and pieces of nature together in coloured cloth. Inside of me is the hope that this untamed beyul in Nepal could somehow serve as a symbol of healing and hope, not just for a community in need, such as the Piikani, where so many children are committing suicide from multigenerational trauma, but for all people everywhere.

I take the braid of sweetgrass and plant my wish inside the Khandro Sanglam. *May we all reconnect with what is most profoundly basic.*

We say goodbye to Tsewang Norbu and begin to trace the line where the green-garden slope meets mountain. We are scrambling up the slope in search of the self-arising images. Sometimes my fingers weave into strong grass for support, and other times I reach for the more definitive purchase of the cliff face. Gargantuan rhubarb leaves form rubbery umbrellas around us. Ani Pema finds wild onions peeking out from a rock ledge. They smell amazing and evoke grumbling in my stomach. I begin to get the distinct impression we're walking through salad. We startle a pheasant and spot a monstrous rodent scuttling across the cliff. We are like children on an adventure, looking for treasure and actually finding it. We crest a flat space where the cliff band forms long, clean faces. Ani Pema spends a long time gazing, trying to find the self-arising images of a sun, moon, drum, *vajra* (symbolic thunderbolt of enlightenment), and other ritual instruments said to be here. She's extremely determined but seems to be having trouble locating them. There is a stone altar with ornate triangular stones placed in offering at the base of the cliff. Who has placed them here? Are there hidden yogis or yoginis in this valley? We leave our own offering, then begin a declining traverse to get back "home." Senge Dongpa Chen punctures the sky above us, still waiting for us to explore her, and watching as we immerse ourselves in her territory. All along the way, Rinzin and Ani Pema sing and laugh. Their eyes spot the chortens near the yak house, and I'm grateful for these earthy features that serve both as spiritual and geographic markers. They point ahead a little, and I see the neon glow of our tents.

But there's a problem. We've made it back, but there's no sign of Tanzin and Tenzin. The sun slides behind the peaks, and our worry builds. Then the sun leaves us in a world of black, and the worry grows intense. How will they get through this terrain in the dark? We decide to eat dinner, and at intervals we take turns exiting the yak house to call out to them and shine lights into the raven sky. But no response. What if one of them has fallen? What if there was a landslide? A broken leg or arm? A slip into a crevasse? I begin making contingency rescue plans. The temperature dips, and the merciless sky opens. I picture them out on the land without a tent, sleeping bag or any means of warmth, now getting soaked in the downpour. And there's nothing we can do. Nothing. Searching for them now would be way too dangerous. Rinzin looks nervous but says that, since there are two of them, they'll be okay. Less than reassured, we eventually decide we must sleep, in case we need to do a rescue tomorrow. I feel guilt as I climb into my sleeping bag, and wish that the warmth could extend to my friends in the dark.

Beyond the Edge of Safety, September 21

Morning breaks, and we gather in the yak house for breakfast. A mouse with powder-grey fur flickers across the stones, taking a brief pause to sniff the remnants of sauce stuck to our bowls. Our team is still down two people. I think of many scenarios. Tanzin and Tenzin have a climbing rope and harnesses, but only Tanzin has climbing experience. The three of us do not have climbing gear. What if we have to cross the glacier, or climb without protection to rescue them? Rinzin offers to go alone and search, but Ani and I firmly disagree and tell him that the three of us must stick together. We agree to wait until 9 a.m., to give them a chance to make it back to camp now that the sun has risen. After that, we'll take the first aid kit and my satellite device and begin searching together over terrain that may be unmanageable. We can use my device to call for a helicopter rescue if needed.

I've asked Tanzin to describe his ordeal in his own words:

My sherpa Tenzin suggested to do a day tour to the stupa, while Ani, Jane and Rinzin visited the gompa, holy caves, and the self-arising images. We left camp in the morning. It was a very clear day after almost a week of rain and cloud. We were all excited about the weather. We had clear views of the stupa from camp, but no one had a clear idea about the route to get there. According to Ani Pema [who was there before the earthquake in 2015], the landscape had changed a lot. She said she had crossed a glacier below our camp, and which is now totally a deep river with no possible way to cross. Our sherpa Rinzin said they used to walk on the glacier that comes from Tashi Palsang to get to Tibet just after winter. He doesn't use the route anymore and says the valley has changed a lot, and that the glacier has retreated.

Our journey started full of excitement and hopes of finding a trail to bring our whole team to the stupa.

Between the two of us we packed one bottle of hot water and two packages of food. I also packed a few leftover pieces of bread that we brought from my home. We climbed to 4530 metres and crossed 3–4 steep rocky ridges standing one after the other. It was super steep! Most of the parts were 95 per cent vertical. Holding grasses and rocks, we were able to cross ridges that dropped 700 to 800 metres to the Sarphu River. After the last one, we could see a big glacier coming from Tashi Palsang. Parts of the glacier had melted, but parts were still active. We descended to the glacier, then connected to each other with rope for safety. We both had normal trekking shoes on, and between us one ice axe. We were not prepared for such a long route, but we were born in the mountains and have worked and lived there most of our lives, and it wasn't our first experience of crossing glaciers without equipment.

On the other side of the glacier there was a steep landslide and junipers. With our rope it became more difficult to cross where the junipers grew. We were very close to the river, which comes from the mountain at the north head of Sarphu. The stupa was 700 to 800 metres above. We looked down valley and could see the land below the gompa and knew that our camp was above it. We thought that, if we could use that route, it would be much shorter and we wouldn't have to climb all the way back over the glacier and ridges. We discussed which route to return by and realized that if we couldn't cross back or get up to the gompa, our journey would become even longer. We finally agreed to take the greater risk of trying for the shorter return route. We started descending to the Sarphu River, which was located at the end of the glacier where the two rivers meet. After 30 minutes' steep descent in loose debris, we made it to the river. Following the water, we found the land below the gompa. We were both very happy. If we'd returned via the same route, it would have taken another six hours from our rest point. We sat by the river and took our lunch. It was 2 p.m. After lunch we started climbing to get to the gompa. It was in shadow. The land was very unstable, and whatever we held onto dislodged. [Side note: this would have been near where Tsewang Norbu showed my group the path down the river, which Ani Pema and I thought was too dangerous.] We climbed about 60 metres. Tenzin was leading the route. He was struggling and telling me that the rock and earth/grass/bushes were unstable, that everything he was trying to hold was loose, and I saw his legs were shaking. I told him to be careful and not fall.

I was holding one small bush that wasn't strong. We were using the same technique of glacier walk I learned during my mountain courses. My one hand was holding the bush, and I used my ice axe, pushing it into the earth. But I realized I couldn't rely on my handholds. If Tenzin fell, and the load went all to my harness, I'm not sure we would have survived. So I used my ice axe to hold my leg and wrapped the rope around my hands (which could have harmed them), but there was no option.

Then Tenzin fell.

He tried to arrest his fall, and I used one hand to stop him. Thankfully, I was able to hold him. We were smiling but full of fear. If we'd fallen to the stones at the river, I'm sure there would've been no chance of surviving. Then I began leading, trying to get up to the gompa, but our minds were not able to cope. We couldn't trust that land. After trying our best, we returned to the Sarphu River. The only option was to return by our original route. We worried how long it would take... We had no more food or energy. It was my first experience like that. Inside I was shaking and feeling very sad, but I smiled to Tenzin. I think he was doing the same – so we could encourage each other. It was 2:45 p.m., and with a big reverse ascent we estimated it would take at least ten hours to get to camp. We knew we must cross the glacier before dark. We weren't talking at all, just walking as fast as possible. I was so tired, just following Tenzin, and we had to stay close because we were roped up. We crossed most of the glacier before dark. Then we had to guess the route. Using our headlamps, we finished crossing the glacier and started up the steep ridges. We could hear sounds coming from the glacier. It was 9 p.m., and we had no more energy left in our bodies. Then it began to rain. Tenzin asked me to go and find a cave to sleep in – we'd seen one about 20 minutes before. But I was worried it might be the shelter of wild animals. So I found one small space in the steep ridge where we could sit. We were so worried; we knew the rest of our team would be waiting for us. We felt badly, but climbing across the ridges at night would mean even more risk. I secured us to the ridge using my ice axe, and we slept in our harnesses. We took off our wet shoes and put our legs into my 60-litre pack.

It became our "sleeping bag," covering until our knees. We shared a single rain poncho over the rest of us.

Time went so slowly. A minute felt like an hour. Somehow we spent the night like that and stayed alive. I couldn't feel parts of my body.

In morning it was difficult to walk. We still couldn't find our way back. It took an hour to find the route we had originally taken. I had no energy left, so Tenzin walked ahead of me and found the trail. I told him to keep climbing and to wait for me at the top. We both wanted to give a message to our friends that we are alive and coming back. Tenzin stayed behind a rock and made some noises so that they could hear, but he didn't want the team to see only him in case they would worry that one of us was injured – or something else. I made it to the top, and we saw them looking our way and waving their hands. We both hid our tears and tried not to look at each other. We began descending toward camp, and Rinzin came up with hot coffee and some food. It was the best I'd ever tasted. My legs couldn't balance me, and I fell down more times than I can count.

Jane and Ani Pema were waiting and very happy to see us. We were so happy to be back too. We both were so sorry for not returning the day before, but we couldn't speak. Jane gave us a hug. We were all hiding our tears. We entered our yak house, warmed our hands and drank tea. Jane, Ani Pema and Rinzin had prepared food for us.

It is a huge feeling of relief to be reunited. Young Tenzin goes to the male tent to recover in his sleeping bag, but Tanzin stays with us, wanting to share the story of what happened. "I don't think anyone can get to the cave and stupa without a big team and lots of gear." As the old man of Gho had said, people "just look at the crystal stupa, make three prostrations, then return."

The day becomes one of rest and recovery for team Tanzin–Tenzin, so Ani Pema and I decide to take the opportunity to wash away the knots of worry that had tied themselves into us. We take the kettle filled with hot water and my "leave no trace" kitchen sink – a collapsible, nylon water bag – and walk down the path to find the stream. Strangely, many of the tributaries have disappeared. We find a small trickle. Ani Pema moves a rock to guide the clear water into a spout so we can fill the water bag. We mix in hot water, which seems like an unprecedented luxury. I strip to my bra and do a deep squat, throwing my locks forward. Ani Pema pours water over my head. I scrub out the oil and smoke, and it feels soooo good. I do the same for Ani Pema, but it's much easier for her. She takes a bar of sandalwood soap and draws it over her scalp. The stubble from her shaved head makes beautiful foam. Next, she washes her bug-bitten thighs, which she's been relentlessly scratching.

Washing in nature like this in the intermittent sunlight feels ridiculously good. The simplicity of warm water and soap takes on elevated status. To brush my hair and work out knots, to put on a little bit of Nivea face cream. To feel the stress of the night unravel.

We spot Tsewang and his puppy near one of the lower ridgeline chortens, and meet him in the yak house for another visit. He tells us this yak house is called Tsewang Gyama Sheer Yak House. We offer him instant Nescafé three-in-one and chat by the open fire while his dog sniffs at our North Face food bag. Tsewang is happy to share information with us, and we are grateful. He explains that there are plans to rebuild the crumbled gompa. The river that flows down Sarphu is called Sarphu Khola on maps, but Tsewang uses the name Chu Na, meaning Black River. This river comes from glaciers high above, and, interestingly, those glaciers also feed the river that flows to Ani Pema's nunnery in Tsum's main valley. The ridge we hope to cross to get to Tashi Palsang he calls Ghongko.

I'm both happy and worried to hear of the renovation plans. On one hand, it shows respect and love for a place held by Tibetan Buddhism as one of the most sacred. On the other hand, and after seeing a sign in the lower part of Sarphu about the trail improvement, I worry what will happen if more travellers come.

I ask Tanzin to translate a question to Tsewang.

"How do you feel about tourists coming here?" I ask. "What if there are more people, and they make garbage?"

Tsewang takes his time to answer. His expression is soft and slack, and there is no tension in his jaw or facial muscles. "It will be nice to see more people because I'm alone," is his reply. I press a little further. "What if tourists and pilgrims change the environment?" But to this, Tsewang replies, "This place is holy, and anyone who wants to come, should." His response is generous, similar to the attitudes of those I met in Morocco's High Atlas Mountains and of the Piikani of Alberta. It's a feeling that land is not owned but rather shared, and that the stories of a land are made rich through people and history. Perhaps he has a trust in the land and the mountain protectors, for he tells us that the yart-sa gunbu (the caterpillar fungus that is being overpicked across the Himalayan high altitudes to supply the Chinese medicine industry) is protected. "The earth here hides them," says Tsewang.

Senge Dongpa Chen, the Lion-Faced Rock, September 22

Padmasambhava, the eighth-century pioneer of Buddhism in Tibet, reasoned that women are better equipped to realize the wisdom of the teachings.

—DAKINI POWER

After Tsewang leaves, time stretches out, long and quiet. There is no mental distraction. I don't even have a book for leisure reading. My mind is vacant and poised, immediate and responsive, soft. Any sense of urgency uncoils, and I let myself continue to dive into a space where time holds less power. Cloud rises up the valley, reaches our elevation, then releases rain. I head to the tent. Tanzin is now sleeping, recovering from his night out on the mountain. I take rest until I notice the rain has stopped. It's late afternoon, and Senge Dongpa Chen begins to sing to me. It's time to climb the ridge to meet the female Buddha who protects this place. It wouldn't take much to believe that she could throw down rocks from her seat of feminine power at the skyline, knocking out anyone with bad intentions. Perhaps that's why Tsewang isn't too worried about disrespectful travellers. He's got backup.

Pulling out the Kyimolung place guide, I prepare myself by reading again about Senge Dongpa Chen.

There is one rock that looks like a lion's head. Stay there and pray to Senge Dongpa Chen. Don't be scared or frightened, act confidently. In the west there is a place that sometimes looks like a lake, sometimes like snow, or like mist. Until you see this place rely on your awareness (rig pa) and pray to Guru Rinpoche. Khandro rock looks like a lion's head: remain there and pray to Senge Dongpa Chen, who owns this place. Thus especially make prayers to her.[28]

Ani Pema and I decide to hike the 470-metre elevation gain together, just the two of us. Tanzin has left his rain pants in the yak house, and Ani Pema sneakily takes them. She laughs as she steps into the legs, making a waterproof layer over her two sets of thermal long johns. She hikes up her robe and stuffs it under her jacket, then shows off her new look to me. Tsewang's puppy has temporarily adopted us. He must have liked what he smelled in our North Face bag. He trails us as we climb.

The grass thins to reveal an almost ocean-like ecosystem. We walk upon a rock garden that blooms with colour, mimicking a coral reef. We climb higher and higher, and then suddenly the puppy gets spooked. He barks wildly, then makes a fast downward retreat.

I look up to the skyline and see the rock standing tall against the erosion that's taken place around her, proud against the scree

---

28 *Place Guide (neyik) for sKyid mo lung (Kymolung) – Valley of Happiness* (translation commissioned by Yeshe Palmo, 2001), 1.

rubble. There is a great gap in the rock, and partway up this gap a massive boulder has been trapped in mid-air. Sky seeps through the openings below and above it, but it just sits suspended in the middle as it has for untold years.

Ani Pema and I trace our way up the rock garden until we crest the pass (4743 metres). My breath pulsates, and my body throbs with delight, so alive in the upper atmosphere. Eric Fabry's translation of the place guide reads: "After that, when you have proceeded to walk, climbed up, and crossed the meadows and pasture lands, and have ascended the...rocky mountain pass, you will access the threshold. And you will arrive at the top of the mountain pass. A singular rock resembling a lion face is present there. In that place of the mountain slope, the female sky dancers (khandros/dakinis) gather and assemble in front of, worship and pray in the presence of the lion faced khandroma, Senge Dongpa Chen."

And now here we are, Ani Pema and I. We've arrived. Our hiking boots touch the thin and bony threshold where land falls away on both sides, the place where Senge Dongpa Chen rock refuses to give way and reaches up instead. Eric asserts that the ridge extending north is thought to be the centre of Kyimolung, though the lamas I've spoken with believe Tashi Palsang is the centre. Either way, some of the treasure texts were revealed at this very location, and are still believed be held within Senge Dongpa Chen's stony protection. There are instructions in the neyig to behave well, to treat the earth with respect, to honour the local people and spirit protectors, to watch your own mind, and to pray to experience a nondual mental state called "emptiness," and what Eric translates as "teachings of pure universal practice devoid of desire." Here in Happy Valley it is all possible.

Clouds move in and enclose the view, smudging out the great peaks beyond, making the moment contain only Senge Dongpa Chen, Ani Pema and me. The rest of the world has been temporarily swallowed. This is feminine ground, and I am here with my Tsumpa sister. She makes an "O" with her lips and pretends to blow away the cloud. She spots a rare flower, royal blue in colour and vibrant like paint pigment. One of the delicate petals has fallen off, so she takes it and places it on her forehead as a blessing, tucking it under her pink plaid headscarf. "Senge blessing." She prays in the mist, and I place one of Ken's offerings among the weathered geography. Just over the Tibet border to the north, the Indigenous Tibetan people face present tense genocide, yet somehow in this deep and hidden valley a paradise remains. At this threshold of stone and sky and cloud, I pray for healing for Indigenous communities that have faced similar violence.

After a time, Ani Pema says, "Let's go around." We retreat a little, then walk the length of Senge Dongpa Chen rock ridge northward. Suddenly, the veil of cloud thins and lifts, and we are left in a world of twilight pinks, purples and empty blues. We sit on the last hump of grass before all land falls away completely, and we are treated to our first glimpse of the vast glacier on the valley floor. It is not crisp, nor white, nor pure. It's a tired and rocky old friend I've known for a thousand years, wise and confident with age, yet slowly disappearing into emptiness as all living things do. It is latticed with moraines. Riddled with debris. We have found the glacial pathway leading to Tashi Palsang, where the body of a Tibetan princess is wrapped up in her mountainous stronghold – though we still can't peek far enough around to see the peak.

We are on a tentacle of land that seems too steep to be properly supported, as it drops hundreds of metres to the ice below. The end of the ridgeline. Yet, here on this precipice, on this dangerous island in the sky, we linger. It is now past 5:30 p.m., and the sun threatens to set, but we can't seem to pull ourselves away from this place. An extra photo, some footage, giggles and an awareness that Ani Pema and I are having a stupendous amount of fun. Sometimes, when things are deemed to be extremely sacred, they become puckered with piousness and too many rules. But here none of that is present. We are pure and lawless. We are women standing strong in the wild, rosy-cheeked and shining. We have not bowed down, but rather we have climbed up, and it feels so very free.

When the moment feels complete, we make a beeline for camp to avoid getting caught in the blackness of night as Tanzin and Tenzin had. We retreat through the alpine grass and pass a milky waterfall. Everything feels feminine in this moment in Senge Dongpa Chen's place. The water itself moves in a voluptuous way as it slides down stone in seductive curves. Eric Fabry found the source of one of the streams we cross, saying it looked like a giant vulva. Now it is dark, and we route find as best we can. Ani Pema detects the faintest signs of trail, the slightest disturbances of flora. We hear a whistle from the darkness, and at first I'm convinced it's a wild bird. But, no, it's Tanzin, who has come to guide us home.

"I guess it's your turn to worry," I tease him.

In the coziness of our tent, Ani Pema and I get tucked in. During the night her sleeping mat deflates, leaving her cold against the ground, and by morning I feel her hugging me for warmth.

Scramble to Camp 3, September 22

Sacred terma are still hidden in the mountains, with some intended for the protection of the earth.[29]

—SERANG MONASTERY, *Bunch of Lotus*

We have seen and experienced so much, and if our trip ends now, I will be able to be content. At least that's what I try to tell myself. But it's not true. It's just not true. When I think about returning now, without quite reaching the heart of the beyul, there is a

---

29 *Bunch of Lotus* notes the treasures that are still hidden: 1) the original 18 Dzogchen Tantras in five cycles written in Lapis given by Vajrapani to King Za; 2) the remains of King Trisong Detsen's youngest son in a copper vessel; 3) Manjusri's diamond sword; 4) Avalokitesvara's crystal rosary; 5) King Trisong Detsen's crown; 6) King Trisong Detsen's robe; and 7) Guru Rinpoche's set of one recitation dagger and 21 action daggers. *Bunch of Lotus: A Commemorative Brochure*, Sangchen Rabten Norbu Ling Foundation, November 2017, 78.

physical and mental discord that tolls like a melancholy bell inside my body. I feel a huge physical urge to walk upon the glacier and bring my eyes into contact with the holy peaks of Tashi Palsang. It's an experience I need to have with my own body, however difficult it may be. Finally, after decades of my heart being one end of a magnet and the heart of Kyimolung the other, the two are ready to snap together and come to rest. Tashi Palsang is just around the corner (albeit a dangerous, risky corner that Tanzin and Tenzin slept on while anchored by an ice axe and harnesses).

The guidebook says, "This place is triangular in shape, the upper part being called Trashi Palzang [Tashi Palsang] also known as Kyi kyi Dzong. In this majestic and fertile place is the daughter of Trisong Detsen [a past king of Tibet], a devata, her body wrapped in clothes along with gold and silver and preserved with medicine. This is a terma of the b[e]yul. Pay your respects to it and leave it as it is."[30] Eric Fabry's translation states, "At the core...cliff faced snow mountain like a chest. It is known as the mountain of Tashi Palzang [Tashi Palsang]...Impressive auspicious glory and brilliance...Guru Rinpoche [Padmasambhava], the seven accomplished masters and knowledge bearers and myself [Rigzin Godem, the tertön who revealed the translated neyig] achieved... realization in this place. Yes, you are into a holy land. That is why you have to journey to the same place to enjoy similar felicity." There are many more treasures listed in the guide that are held within Tashi Palsang, such as Buddha relics, a vase from which there is a continual flow of long-life water, the body of a child prince, the lion throne of the Tibetan King Trisong Detsen, 500 scrolls of Vajrayana Chinese texts translated into Tibetan that must be carried on the backs of seven men, Yeshe Tsogyal's[31] necklaces and ornaments, sacred teachings, an elixir of immortality,

---

30 *Place Guide (neyik) for sKyid mo lung (Kymolung) – Valley of Happiness* (translation commissioned by Yeshe Palmo, 2001), 12.

31 Yeshe Tsogyal is Padmasambhava's consort, and she hid many of the treasures in different beyul.

and substances to obtain bliss – all of which must be left untouched, inside the mountain. (I can't write all the treasures in this book because there are too many!)

We wake to rain and talk about spending one more night where we are at Camp 2, then hiking out due to the bad weather, but I sit and will the weather to cooperate. At 11 a.m. the heavy sky seals the rain just long enough for us to break camp. "Let's go up!" I urge. We stuff our tents and sleeping bags into their respective sacks, pack just enough food for one night at the glacier, then begin the most gruelling and nerve-wracking part of our adventure.

We trace Tanzin's exploratory route, working our way across and over multiple tendinous ridges. The climb is stiff, slippery and cold. It involves several technical climbing moves where we must find footholds and handholds in the stone, or, failing that, hardy grass and shrubs. At times, these gifts of vegetation are the only thing preventing us from plummeting down huge chutes. Our hands turn puffy, red and numb. This ethereal route to Tashi Palsang demands total awareness. We cling to the tiniest bits of earth, with sky above and a sea of cloud below.

Despite the level of exposure, I feel confident in how my group can read the land as they watch for handholds and the dangers of loose stone, and I sense us all observing each other, at the ready in case anyone loses contact. At one point, Tanzin says, "It's good that it's cloudy. Much less scary because you can't see what's below. It's about an 800-metre drop here." Thankfully, he told me this *after* I'd made it across. He'd also told me earlier that, no, this part is not *too* dangerous, but that one must be sure of every footstep *all the time*. The movement to Tashi Palsang becomes a pure form of meditation. My mind is in a flow state as it bridges the connection between this paradisiacal yet physical environment with my own body. The consequences are dire and real. If I lose concentration, I could lose my life. In Yeshe's master's thesis, she writes that the place guides/neyigs give a vision of a wonderful place of great potential for those seeking realization, but that it isn't a quick or easy path. Boy, was she right.

As we climb, I'm conscious I could never do this alone. I need Tanzin's mountain training, route finding and first aid and emergency knowledge. I need Ani Pema's spiritual connection, her prayers and offerings, her laughter. I need Rinzin's on-the-ground knowledge of this landscape, and I also need young Tenzin's watchful eyes as he takes on the main role of spotting me. At one point, it feels like we've become spiders, delicately shifting our feet and hands along tiny pockets that imprint the vertical stone. We thrust our hips to the cliff. Beneath, only vapour. Together, this adventure works. Together, we move toward the holy mountain, whose girth and height is so massive we can feel it before we see it.

The way often looks completely impossible, and the scale too grand for my Albertan brain to fathom. Just when it looks like we'll need ropes to continue, we somehow find a way to progress. At one point, I find myself slinging one leg over the top of a ridge so I'm straddling it as if riding a horse, then flinging the other leg to the other side to continue on. My body acts spontaneously; my toe makes a slight pivot on a nubbin of rock, my fingers braid into grass for support. Every cell inside of me is awake and adaptive.

We find a rare prickly blue poppy emerging from a rock outcrop that gets the Tsumpas talking. Its beauty fascinates them. It has vibrant blue petals like tissue paper. The stamens at its centre are the colour of the type of sunshine that a child draws, and the leaves and buds are covered in protective hair. The neyig says there are many unique mountain flowers here that "shine and glitter."[32]

My adrenaline has been flowing in a slow and steady river inside my body. I need it to keep me clear and aware of each step, as Tanzin wisely instructed, yet my body now feels the need to release such intense concentration. No such luck, as we have more ribs to cross. It's as if I'm taking a math exam for six hours straight.

We can feel the icy sheet of the glacier now, but it is hidden by cloud. We search for a place to pitch camp beside it, but we can't find water. Even though we're soaked through, and the freezing

---

32 Eric Fabry's translation.

rain is relentless, what we need is a stream outlet so we can make hot drinks and food. We struggle for a while as we decide where to set down our gear, and then the clouds part just long enough for us to see a stream. Rinzin forges ahead to collect water, while we retreat to a grassy saddle slung across the cloudy abyss – the only flat ground around. We use our slow, swollen fingers to click metal tent poles into place, and erect our tents side by side. Then we hike to the outside edge of the saddle, where a stone outcrop pokes up, and hang a tarp. We huddle underneath at odd angles, like a family of monkeys sheltering from rain, then boil water, drink coffee and make vegetable soup. I'm shivery and shaky, not just from the temperature but also the effects of post-adrenaline. My kidneys feel worked. I have inner worries that this was way too intense; that I've pushed us too far. If anything happens back here, we're in serious trouble. We take time to warm our hands on our metal cups, and to let the excitement settle.

"We can eat in our tents tonight," says Tanzin. Here we don't have the "luxury" of a yak hut. We are fully solo, relying only on what we've managed to haul up the mountain.

We retreat to the warmth of our sleeping bags for rest. Ani is beside me; our bodies eventually unclench from the cold and the grip of basic survival. She pulls out her phone and plays a recording of her voice. It's a familiar chant, one I heard when we met in 2012. Back then, my dear friend Lopsang and I had hiked up to her nunnery. We arrived just as night fell, and she was closing herself inside the gompa for her evening ritual. She directed us to sit, then began a slow, rhythmic chant. She was the only nun at Drephuet Dronme at the time, alone in that great high place. Her strong, slightly gritty voice filled the dark nunnery and brought it to life. She struck a bell and beat a large drum, and during her ritual I moved closer to an empty throne near the front altar. The throne held a photo of the previous incarnation of my teacher – one of the few existing photos of the 16th Drakar Rinpoche, who passed away in 1959 as the Chinese Army invaded his monastery in Tibet.

The haunting ritual she performed that night was called *chöd*, in which the yogini envisions offering her own flesh to demons. By giving away pieces of one's body, it allows a severing from attachment to the confines of human form. It's a practice aimed at destroying the strange sense of ego we humans seem to have, the idea that we are so separate from others. The practitioner feels great compassion for the demons, who are suffering, and shares something of herself. Now, in our tent at the heart of Kyimolung, she plays her own voice chanting chöd once again, and I get lost in the vibrations. Chöd practitioners are traditionally those who meditate in cremation grounds and wild, lonely places. They blow through human thigh bone trumpets and wear bone ornaments like Senge Dongpa Chen to remind them of the impermanence of life. If Ani Pema does indeed decide to do a three-year retreat, this is the topic she wants to meditate on. Ani Pema is a woman of this land. She is a woman in her own skin. There is nowhere else I want to be right now except right here with her. I rest on the earth. I rest with my friend. I listen to the curls of sound that spread from her phone to make contact with the grass, rock and sky, and I delight in having shed my own layers of self to be so naked and honest in Shangri-La.

Being Canadian, I have been trained to never, ever, at any cost, have any food inside my tent. Not even toothpaste. Not even deodorant. (Not that I currently have either of those things with me anyway.) Our black and grizzly bears are keen sniffers. Normally, when I'm random camping I must gather my food into bear-proof bags and hike it at least 100 metres away. I always put it much further for peace of mind. When young Tenzin calls at our tent door, and passes us packages of freeze-dried food and spoons, I'm elated. We put the food on my side beneath the fly to let it soften inside the pouch.

Soon I hear something strange. A bubbling sound.

"Ani, what's that sound?" I ask, my ears straining, eyes searching. She points to the food. I open the tent to inspect it.

"Careful. Hot!" she warns.

I inspect her bag of food, which is now rumbling at a full boil. What is happening here? Steam escapes out a small hole in the bag as the food cooks itself. Reading the bag, I see that it says, "Korean self heat and cook."

"How does it do that?" I wonder aloud. After ten minutes, she opens the bag to reveal fluffy rice and soft veggies, and she digs in, enjoying her meal. The package contains an inner chamber of food, and the outer metal package holds a small pouch. When the pouch makes contact with cold water, something magical happens and the water comes to a boil. I'm blown away by this amazing technology and wonder when it will come to Canada.

The boys are nearby in their green tent, singing melodic Nepali songs. Their voices are smooth honey in this high and holy place. Accompanying percussion comes from the glacier itself, which moans and grinds and lets off rockfall. I sense it as an alive thing, a time capsule connecting us to the beyul origin stories of the 700s and the much older history of mountains being formed, of ice ages coming and going, of creation and destruction.

"Tibetan calendar," says Ani Pema, as she extends her phone for me to look at. I realize that tomorrow will be my 39th birthday. The Tibetan calendar shows that it will be an auspicious day, and the inspirational quote says, "Happiness is shared." Ani takes a few selfies on her phone, and then we drift into sleep, curled up together like sisters, while our brothers become quiet in the tent next to us and dream their own dreams.

The Heart of the Beyul, September 23

"Happy Birthday, Jane!" Tanzin calls out from his tent.

"Thank you, Tanzin!"

I'm turning 39 years old at the climax of our trip. I press the tent zipper between thumb and finger, pull open the fly and see blue sky above. It's the best birthday present ever! The weather that enclosed us yesterday has been inhaled by space. I lace my stiff, wet boots (how they hurt!) and do a walkabout to take in a whole new landscape. What we couldn't see yesterday is now revealed.

Tanzin has picked the most beautiful campsite. Our tents are sheltered in a wee saddle above the glacier. Just enough grass has crept over the stone to make the earth soft here, but we are surrounded by the bony sharpness of the high alpine. Peaks proudly display their majesty in the early morning light. It has snowed above us, and the peaks gleam white. I spot a different species of wild rhubarb (the Tsumpas call it *yay-jua*) growing in the struggling green, blunted from its high elevation home.

Everyone else is still in their tents. I walk to a private place beyond their view. I let myself be soaked into all I see, and I sing the special song Yeshe gave me – the "Pigeon Song," by Milarepa. One line of the song says, "The sixfold collection of consciousnesses [referring to our senses of touch, taste, smell, etc.] is lucid right there in itself." Right now, this land is the Buddha, and by setting my eyes on it directly, by smelling the glacial breeze, hearing the shifting rock and feeling the last of the night's cold bite at my toes, I am directly experiencing it. There was no shortcut to arrive here. It required intense effort and now being lucid, open, and myself in this place. That means I'm here with all my human hang-ups and imperfections and emotions – and yet I'm leaving them to play at their own game while I dwell in the magnitude of the moment.

I pop my head into the boys' tent like a kid at Christmas, saying, "Let's go explore the glacier!" I cannot leave Kyimolung without seeing Tashi Palsang, and she's just around the protective spur we slept on. We are so very close. The sky toys with me a little by showing patches of sapphire, then filling with porous cloud, which I fear will grow to swamp out possible views. We do not have enough food to linger another night. This is it. It's now or never.

We traverse across loose scree to the gravelly moraine. Not a single tree exists up here in the big wide open. We gingerly climb over the glacier to its middle, avoiding crevasses that project downward to reveal its inner workings. It is so layered: on the surface, it is debris-covered and earthy; the middle is constructed of icy-white vertical shears; the bottom, dark and mysterious, as if it has no bottom at all. We hear it moan, press and move.

Rinzin points out the route he used to take to Tibet. "There is so much erosion now," he observes. Sections of earth the size of high-rise buildings have tumbled down, leaving gashes in the land like open wounds. He tells us that he would not use this route again, and that he currently uses a route just west in the valley of Nubri. He says the glacier used to curl much farther down valley, and we wonder about climate change and its drastic effect on this sensitive environment.

Looking down valley to the point of the great curve that leads to the gompa, we have a stunning view of the wall of mountains that holds the self-arising stupa. From this vantage point, we can see its location, but not the stupa itself. It is flanked by red and white waterfalls – Technicolor nature. Tanzin ponders the view. "Even on Everest, there are not views like this," he says.

I turn 180 degrees to allow myself to experience what I have longed for. My eyes start at my boots. The glacier where I stand is brown and in the process of dying. My eyes trace it as it rises higher to where it makes a stark transition to clean white. Then it bumps into the walls of the Sringi Himal Range, where cliffs rise to form peaks. The one that tickles the sky at 7100 metres is Tashi Palsang. Hello, Tashi Palsang.

This formidable peak is not static or still. She is active and sends down avalanches before our eyes. We watch white sluff tumble down her walls. The noise echoes off the stone and dances inside our ears. This place feels conscious. We are in the midst of a great geological history, and we are at the beating, resonant heart of Kyimolung beyul. It's like we are discovering the great pyramids of Egypt – Himalayan style.

According to the guidebook, somewhere in the stronghold of the mountain "there is a door, locked by molten metal. Inside there is a cave held up by two pillars. There is terma in this cave...The terma must not be taken out. If you offer on auspicious days, the teachings will flourish and the king's ancestors will arise and the country will be blessed and all will be auspicious."[33] We could spend much time searching for this cave and for the treasures within. How incredible it would be to find the body of a Tibetan princess, or water that grants immortality. Teachings that lead to enlightenment.

But we do not.

"People believe that this mountain is so sacred you shouldn't touch it," says Tanzin, and I recall the monks in Serang Monastery on the other side who threatened violence to the climbers who wanted to summit her. The neyig says you should connect yourself with this sacred place and be ready to be possessed by it, that the treasures and the earth must be protected, and that only through this type of harmony can one actually enter the beyul. Today, we are amid profound history. We have sweated and embraced fear openly, and we have stripped off layers of adulthood to play in the mountains together. It has been physically demanding, but every place I'd read about and hoped to find I've found.

We explore in slow motion in the warm sunshine. There is so much texture here. There are so many surfaces and prism-like aspects. Rinzin lies down on his belly to receive the warmth that has accumulated in the rocks. Tanzin is down to his favourite navy blue T-shirt, and his skin soaks up sunbeams. He spreads out his clothes and naps in the clean light. Ani Pema takes photos. I sit and stare at Tashi Palsang, and she grants me brief views of her boundaries and the border between her form and the thin atmosphere, then teases with more cloud. My eyes trace her lines and her vertical folds, taking in a view reserved for wandering meditators, tertöns, the bravest nomads and, now, me.

---

33 *Place Guide (neyik) for sKyid mo lung (Kymolung) – Valley of Happiness* (translation commissioned by Yeshe Palmo, 2001), 4.

I consider the auspiciousness of this moment and take time to reflect. When I travelled to Tsum in 2017, leading a group of trekkers, on what was to be our last day, I woke up early. I was extremely excited because my friend the 17th Drakar Rinpoche had walked up the mountains to meet me. He hadn't been to his home village in Tsum for years, and I was deeply touched he'd made such effort. But, unfortunately, I woke up sick. I began retching up absolutely everything in my stomach. I began to cry, not only because I felt horrible, but because my travel group was set to fly out by helicopter that night. My time with Rinpoche would be wasted as I hung my head over a pit toilet. I dragged myself to his family home to spend time with him in my sorry state, sometimes excusing myself to clamber down his wooden ladder, wobble past a scary mastiff and vomit into the toilet yet again. It was a paradox: I was with my teacher in his birthplace – a peak experience – yet I was also experiencing a pretty disgusting aspect of being human.

He must have appreciated my effort, for he came to the guest house where our crew was staged, until two helicopters would return us to Kathmandu. The last thing I wanted to do was get on a helicopter and leave my friend. My mom and the trekkers I'd brought on the trip put me in a room, and I lay there on a bed, listening to gale-force winds funnelling through Tsum Valley. I became delirious from whatever bug had entered my system. I was in a state between sleep and wakefulness. I watched the floral curtains shift in the wind that snuck through the cracks of the window glass. The roar of the first helicopter echoed in my head, and then I knew my mom was gone. Then I heard the second helicopter was delayed until the next day. All the while I heard Rinpoche just outside my door, chatting with the two remaining trekkers. His voice was like a song to me.

In my state of delirium and dehydration, I began to have visions. This has never happened to me before. Great golden Buddhas danced in my mind, and then the Buddhist image of swastikas began forming on their hands and foreheads. I knew a little bit about the swastika image – which was later perverted by the Nazis – but I didn't really know its meaning. Much later, after I was safely back in Canada, I learned that they represent auspiciousness. Yeshe told me that, when she did her retreat, she would sit upon one placed under her cushion, and that it represented unmovable stability.

This trip to Sarphu, a deeper penetration into Kyimolung than my previous trips, has had no special dreams or visions. It has been simple, spontaneous, intense and fun. But I can't help wondering if those dreams I had when I was reluctantly leaving Tsum in 2017 were a signal of the auspiciousness we've just experienced in reaching Tashi Palsang. Great auspiciousness indeed.

As I walk the ice, I have the rare experience of being completely satiated. We have achieved our goals. So many factors had to come into play for this moment to occur: Yeshe's gruelling travels to Kyimolung, her thesis and then her willingness to share such sacred work. The work of other scholars, and the openness of the lamas to share their texts and stories. Ani Pema's prayers and friendship, and her powerful personality. Tanzin's mountain skills, and the bravery that comes from being 27 years old. My family's loving support, and my past trips that have given me knowledge and fortitude. The weather, too, for though it has been rainy and almost always uncomfortable, the sky kept parting just when we needed it to. If we'd come in spring, this place would be choked with snow. If we'd waited until the clarity of late autumn, the waterfalls that leak down the mountainsides would be frozen, making it far too treacherous to traverse the great ridges. We've been given a great gift – the story from Padmasambhava's treasure texts. How wonderful that, so long ago, someone like him would think into the future and plant the seeds of a great adventure such as this. Thank you, Guru Rinpoche.

I notice that, while I feel complete, I do not feel high. The experience is really quite simple. There is no sudden enlightenment, no flash of insight, no cascading bliss. I'm here with my regular neurosis and subconscious self-loathing, with my hopes and fears, with myself. I feel complete, but I'm not in a Nirvana that's separate from who I really am. One might think that making it to the heart of the beyul could solve all the mental problems of the human mind. But, for me, it's not like that. In my lineage, there's a thing called *ordinary mind*. The magazine *Lion's Roar* explains it like this:

> From the Mahamudra point of view, the nature of our mind is completely enlightened right from the beginning, and it is known as ordinary mind. In this context, "ordinary" does not refer to mundane consciousness – a mind that is totally caught up in this world of samsara. Ordinary mind refers to mind that is not fabricated in any way. It is the natural or fundamental state of our mind, totally free from all conceptual elaborations. It is the best part of mind. When we experience this ordinary mind, we experience buddha mind.[34]

I look at this moment openly and know the grass, the cold, the excitement and the love I feel here for my friends and myself in an immediate and vulnerable way.

We have followed the map. We have found terma sites and sacred locations. We stand at this secret side of Tashi Palsang, and our wishes have been fulfilled.

I deposit the last of Ken's Blackfoot/Soki-tapi offerings, and Ani Pema extracts herbal offerings from her clothes and lights the dry fibres. The wind and the mountains receive.

We pack up Camp 3 and retreat to the yak house over the same challenging ground. During our journey, Ani Pema has been discovering incense herbs proliferating the alpine slopes, such as juniper, a leathery leafed plant she calls *ballu*, and a mossy silver ground cover that smells amazing when you press it between your fingers. She takes some from her pockets, and we place it inside a

---

34 Dzogchen Ponlop Rinpohe, "Pointing Out Ordinary Mind," *Lion's Roar*, August 15, 2018, https://www.lionsroar.com/pointing-out-ordinary-mind/.

bag to send back to Ken and his foster boys, so their offerings can be replenished.

It seems that Kyimolung beyul has truly served its intergenerational purpose. Padmasambhava's intention for the hidden valleys was to offer pockets of refuge. He wrote a prediction that Tibet would be invaded, its people decimated, its monasteries destroyed and the lineage of its kings threatened. Yet even though we could walk right now into Tibet distance-wise, to where genocide was undertaken by the Chinese government, where border monasteries like my friend Drakar Rinpoche's Drakar Taso Monastery were ripped apart, spiritual texts scattered across the earth, monks and nuns murdered and lay people forced into labour camps, Kyimolung has remained safe from destruction. Kyimolung became a place where Tibetans fled for refuge.

The Indigenous Peoples of Alberta and North and South America did not have hidden valleys for their artifacts and rituals, and the Amazigh people of Ait Bougemez weren't even allowed to give their children Indigenous names until recently, being forced instead to use the Arabic names of the majority. This contrast shows the power of the concept of beyul. These safe pockets can offer hope, happiness and protection in a world that's so mixed up and power hungry it's destroying itself. In them, we can be safe being who we really are. Submission is only to the demands of the land and the understanding of the mental constructs that so often hold us captive, ones we can break free of if we work at it.

Parting with Ani Pema, September 24

Today, we begin our descent from Kyimolung's core. First, we deep clean Tsewang's yak house to erase the signs of our inhabitance. Tanzin leaves a tarp as a gift. We tried multiple times to offer Tsewang money for the firewood we used, but he adamantly refused. I leave some anyway, tucking Nepali rupees into a safe place for him to find. Then I choose a few lacy flowers and place them at the entrance. The porters seal the hut with the stone slab, and we depart.

We climb to the high pass where the prayer flags flutter, and Ani Pema pulls out a white kata and a pen. In Tibetan script, she writes each of our names upon the fabric. We will hang this kata with the prayer flags so our names, pieces of ourselves, can float in this valley of happiness.

I make a request. "Ani Pema, can you please write Yeshe Palmo on the kata?" Yeshe has been with us all along, and her work was a great trailblazer, allowing us to pass into Sarphu with heightened awareness. Though she's in Scotland now, living with leukemia, she was also with me every time I reached into my pack to cross-check her map and translations. With her name alongside ours, Tanzin climbs up on Tenzin's shoulders and ties the kata to the flags.

Tsewang recommended we take a high route out of Sarphu. The trail takes us to the toe of another of Sringi Himal's glaciers. There is a story about this place. It's said that a poacher once came in search of animals to hunt. Here he found a portal into the beyul. He was extremely excited and went to get his family to show them, but when he returned, the door had closed. They say it was due to his karma. By taking the lives of animals, he wasn't able to access the beyul. This belief in nonviolence is integral to beyul lore.

We descend from the glacial zone toward a yak camp called Karche. There are so many herbs and flowers here it's like being in a garden. Tanzin finds tiny blueberries that glow like neon bulbs.

We reach Camp 1 beneath the orange cliffs. Our bodies are strong from the time spent at high altitude and from life lived outdoors. We almost fly across the terrain, moving from glacier to subalpine to jungle, and then the emerald bamboo forest shelters us with its verdancy. We press our boots into seductive dirt. We walk for about ten hours, descending over 2000 metres to the main valley. When Tanzin checks his iPhone health app, it tells us we've covered about 28 kilometres.

We stumble into Gho village in the main Tsum Valley, where a week ago we'd scrutinized maps and worried about ever finding the alluring points in the place guide. Our bodies are tired, but our minds are elated. Somehow we have energy to wash. Tanzin brings me a bucket of hot water, and I go to the shower room (a concrete floor beside the pit toilet). I remove my dirt-encrusted clothes, then pour steaming water over my body. I lather up, loving the feeling of slick soap over my skin and the smell of coconut. Finally, I dump the bucket over my head and am washed clean. My poor body has been through many ecosystems all within one day. Yet I feel strong and alive.

The boys wash outside at a black holding tank. Tenzin has his shirt off. He is skinny and incredibly strong, and his muscles flicker on and off as he scrubs. Rinzin walks by, shining and clean but still wearing dirty clothes, as we all must.

"Clean on the inside, but not on the outside. Seventy per cent clean!" Tanzin calls out.

This is our last night together as a group. We eat big meals of dal bhat to nourish ourselves after all the freeze-dried food. It feels as if months passed while we were in Sarphu, or years, even another life lived while inside Kyimolung's potent stronghold. Rinzin sits beside me, his brown eyes glowing. He gets Tanzin to translate a message to me, saying how much he enjoyed the trip and the company. Ani Pema says that she is so happy she got to spend more time in Sarphu. The previous time, 12 years prior, she went to the gompa, but couldn't see the stupa due to cloud. Now her pilgrimage has been fulfilled. There is the general feeling of relief at being back from a great and dangerous adventure, at having realized every possible wish. The text itself says that people who venture to the heart of Kyimolung and find it "will have all their purposes accomplished...in both this life and the next."[35] I

---

35 *Place Guide (neyik) for sKyid mo lung (Kymolung) – Valley of Happiness* (translation commissioned by Yeshe Palmo, 2001), 2.

feel a settled joy. The ending of an old karmic tale has finally been scribed into my bones.

Ani Pema and I retreat to our twin beds in the guest house. She does prostrations on her bed, almost hitting her head on a ceiling beam. I can't help but wonder if this is the place where we got our flea bites, so instead of using the enticing cotton bedding that appears to be clean, I climb into my filthy (yet familiar) sleeping bag. We sleep so hard.

Trek to the Western Gate, September 25

Today we must part. Ani Pema will follow the main trail to upper Tsum to resume her duties. Rinzin will go with her as far as Lamagaun to return our tents, then he will hike down valley to his village. Tenzin will stay with us as my porter as we make our way west to Nubri and to Earth's eighth-highest mountain: Manaslu. This region is the western part of Kyimolung, the western petals of the lotus, and an area I have never explored.

Ani Pema sits on her twin bed, quiet in the morning light. I wordlessly pack up my gear and check the status of our wet socks on the line outside (still wet). She continues to sit, then begins rubbing her throat.

"Are you okay?" I ask. Her face is solemn.

"Yes." She continues to rub her throat.

"Is your throat sore? Pain? I have some medicine…"

She is silent a moment, then says, "I little bit sad. Today I go up, you go down." Then tears wet her eyes. I put my arms around her and say, "I know." Then I walk to the veranda, take a few deep breaths and burst into tears. They flow so fast, hot and ugly that I have to go back into our room to hide from the people milling about the courtyard.

"Ani! You made me cry!" I say between sobs. I don't know when I'll see my Tsum sister again. My children are approaching post-secondary, and I cannot financially justify more trips to Tsum in the near future. Ani Pema may retreat from the outer world into the meditative world of chöd practice. We don't know when we'll see each other again.

Breakfast is eaten mostly in silence. We say our goodbyes in the courtyard, but Ani Pema barely looks at me. We don't get one last hug, as public displays of affection aren't common in the Himalayas. I look to see Ani Pema and Rinzin on the trail that leads into the world I dream about, the world where I left part of myself years ago, a world I don't know when I will see again, and then they disappear behind a great wall of rock.

Tanzin, Tenzin and I begin the descent out of Tsum Valley. We take a rest at a guest house in a village called Chumling, which I first visited in 2012. So much has changed; a large, new addition has been appended onto what was once a very simple structure where I had slept. The guest house owner recognizes me. I have a photo of him that looks like it's straight out of a *National Geographic* magazine, or even from 100 years ago – it's hard to tell its vintage as he squats low by his fire in the early winter light. Now the man looks trekking savvy. The trekking industry in Tsum has boomed since my first visit. Tsum is still very protected, but it has undeniably been "discovered." A large ring of keys jingles from the proprietor's belt as he commands the construction workers. I'm quite sure that layperson status in Tsum must be directly connected to the number of keys on one's belt. Lama Pasang in Lamagaun also had an impressive number that made music when he walked.

"How was Sarphu?" asks the owner, though we don't know how he heard about our journey. Word of our adventure has spread through the village grapevine.

His wife sits on a tarp sorting grain. Workers mill about, and I see one who is transgender. It's the first time I've seen someone who doesn't fit into the traditional gender roles here. This person has the strong legs of a porter – the calf muscles are lined and responsive to each step – and wears a headband and a tight T-shirt and has a distinctly feminine chest and gait. Tanzin warmly shakes their hand, which makes me smile.

As we drink coffee and eat noodles, the owner feeds his dog pieces of meat from some animal's jawbone. He shares the meat with his wife, while he himself chews a morsel of gristle. It is late morning; flies wake up and buzz about us.

After our rest, Tanzin delivers bad news. Tenzin's mother is extremely sick with a massive headache and is being cared for in our clinic. His family has sent word to this guest house owner that he must return to his village immediately so he and his mom can be evacuated by helicopter to Kathmandu. Tanzin deliberately ensured that his porter got a good meal before telling him the news. Tanzin and I take all extraneous gear from our packs and give it to Tenzin to take down in the helicopter, say our goodbyes and hope for the fast recovery of Tenzin's mom. It's just the two of us now, with our heavy packs and no porter. My pack sits on a plastic chair, looking like it was at an all-you-can-eat gear buffet, its plump red nylon stressing the seams. I wonder what lugging it over the impending 5106-metre Larkye Pass will feel like.

Tanzin and I hike down to Lokpa village, the first village in lower Tsum. We sit with the village Chief and have a chat in the hot afternoon sun. Tanzin is well connected. There's a photo of him with the Chief's son hanging proudly on the guest house wall. Tanzin comes from a long lineage of famous lamas in upper Tsum; he himself is related to the great treasure finder Guru Chowang. These connections allow us to get great rooms in all the guest houses, and I am brought closer to the local culture than the groups who come with trekking guides who only started coming to Tsum when the government opened it to tourism in 2008.

News of our adventure has spread even here in Lokpa, the lowest part of Tsum, and the Chief asks us about our expedition. He tells us that a great Tsum lama (Drukpa Rinpoche) requested that his ward make it possible for more people to visit Sarphu. The Chief has already spent a lot of money on trail improvements (which we saw and experienced from the Eastern Gate of Kyimolung), and he asks us how the trail was. Tanzin honestly tells him he has a long way to go yet (the improvements were only visible in the jungle lowlands). He tells us that previous generations travelled to the abandoned gompa via the glacier. This oral history helps confirm the great glacial retreat we experienced and the effects of climate change. Our route was much harder than hiking along the valley bottom; we had to become monkeys and climb over ravine walls and across mountain flanks instead.

After the wild abyss of Sarphu, I'm faced with a strange acclimatization process. I'm no longer the only inji. I feel jangled by the other travellers and languages I hear, so I retreat to my bedroom, which has three single beds but only one Jane. I miss Ani Pema's presence and feel strangely exposed. I listen to music and try to let my mind re-balance in these different surroundings.

Toward the Western Gate

Nubri and the Manaslu Circuit, September 26

Today, we leave Tsum. We descend rapidly, then pass through a new entrance/exit gate. Red pillars shine in the jungle, and I feel I'm in an Asian scroll painting. A sign displays the rules of nonviolence that govern this valley. This year marks the centennial anniversary of the signing of the pact. The beneficial effects of nonviolence are clear – Tsum Valley has even won a World Wildlife Federation Nepal Conservation Award for the vision of its forefathers.[36]

---

36 See https://ntnc.org.np/news/mcaps-sakya-committee-receives-wwf-nepal-conservation-award.

We find the junction of the Shyar Khola and Budhi Gandaki rivers. The eastern path is the one we've come down from Tsum. The western branch reaches to Nubri and the Manaslu Circuit, a famous trekking route that skirts Earth's eighth-highest mountain, Mount Manaslu (8163 metres). I've never been this way before. On previous treks I've either retraced my steps or helicoptered out of Tsum. But, back home, Mike had encouraged me to take this longer loop, even though it will add a week to my time away. He thought it would be a good way for me to process all I'd been through in Sarphu and to do something fun. Yup. Mike is that amazing. It will also give me the chance to make a seldom done side trip to Serang Valley in Nubri, another power place of the beyul that will grant us views of the opposite side of Tashi Palsang. I'll be adding over 100 kilometres to my Sarphu/Tsum expedition.

The lotus shape of Kyimolung beyul spreads all across this region. As mentioned before, it has gates through which one can enter, and we had been through the Eastern Gate in Sarphu Valley. The place guide states, "East, there is a door of water and rock. The south door is rock and trees. The west door is rock and wind. The north door is rock and snow."[37] Three gates can be reliably identified in the neyig, but the Western Gate of rock and wind is still a mystery. There is still much for us to explore and discover.

I become aware of a strange divide as I reinsert myself into the trekking scene. At lunch, I notice that trekkers hang out with each other while the guides and porters eat in the "Nepali" kitchens. I'm without my Tsumpa brigade, and I am a solo trekker. Tanzin is inside, and I'm outside with people from Germany and the United States. I feel a little in-between – not totally foreign trekker, not totally Tsumpa. I'm happy when Tanzin invites me inside.

Tanzin senses my preference for off-the-beaten-track places and my seeming lack of need for comfort, so instead of sleeping at a guest house on the main trekking route, he takes me to

---

37 *Place Guide (neyik) for sKyid mo lung (Kymolung) – Valley of Happiness* (translation commissioned by Yeshe Palmo, 2001), 1.

Bihi Pedhi, a village higher above the fast-flowing Budhi Gandaki River. All around is a mind-blowing diversity of edible foods. Veggies and grains sprout from every possible nook and cranny of the land and the villagers' gardens. We find a guest house, and inside I spot a storage room filled two feet high with cobs of corn. A plump squash sits nearby, waiting to be chopped into a curry, and Tanzin and I sit at a long table with yet another ward Chief, while his wife cuts up a cucumber so gigantic they have to tell me it's a cucumber. The outside garden has a basil plant as big as a bush, cauliflowers, carrots and squash vines whose green tendrils clasp the surrounding stone fence and lace it with green. The cliffs above have been hewn into terraces to increase the arable land. The village is a hive of harvesting activity. People pound grain and collect seed in the open air. One woman does this with a chubby baby wrapped to her back. The scene is undeniably happy and healthy, and I think of how, in Edmonton, I don't even know the names of many of my neighbours.

Tanzin chats with the Chief, a robust and extroverted man wearing impressive knock-off trekking pants. He tells us of a locals' route to Serang Valley, which will be steeper but shorter. Next year, he says, a new suspension bridge will be built, making the long trek to Serang much more accessible. The Chiefs and the people they represent seem hungry for change and development. For centuries, Tsum and Nubri evolved at a traditional pace. Now trekking and Wi-Fi are facilitating lightning speed advancement. Local people want more comfort and connection, and I totally understand their desires (I benefit from such comforts in my home in Canada). These changes allow our clinic and school unprecedented access to information, and we can take nimble, life-saving action when needed. But I do feel something akin to grief. It was the hard path to Tsum that helped my own spiritual journey bear fruit.

I climb to the rooftop to ponder all this. The sun has dropped behind the mountain walls, and the air has turned silver grey. I put on my pink down jacket and settle myself onto a bench. Pieces of rebar sprout up all around me on this unfinished concrete rooftop. In the space of contemplation, I realize I have none, absolutely none, of the anxiety I bear at home. My chest no longer has stabbing pains and pressure, and my mental pace has slowed. It's as if my nervous system is matching the environment. There's a sense of expanded time here. The locals believe that if things don't happen in this life, they'll happen in the next, and that sentiment creates a feeling of contentment and a tendency away from rushing. Things here are not perfect, nor are they easy. It's physically gruelling, and I never quite know what door to open or what stone passageway I should walk down to eventually find the squat toilet, where I'll never exactly know just what to do with my toilet paper. My hair is oily and dusty, and my socks haven't been washed in weeks. Yet, despite the perceived hardships, the anxiety is gone.

I look to a stone house and see a man there. He smiles and waves, and though we are strangers, I feel he's my brother. Village life binds and connects people in a way I find deeply supportive. There's always someone you know at the ready to help if you're sick. If you need help planting seed. If your spouse passes away. When you get old. No one is left to suffer alone, whether mentally or physically, and you can feel that support vividly here. Whereas, at home, there is a great isolation, even when among others.

The flip side is that there's a serious lack of privacy. Everything is public. Even news of our journey to Sarphu had gone down the Tsum grapevine, greeting us at villages before we'd even arrived. Villagers wash at public fountains and drop in on each other's homes unannounced and often. And I have no idea where and how people have sex, since families generally sleep in the same room.

After nightfall, we gather in the kitchen to sit with the Chief, a very drunk young man who has trouble holding up his head, and two traders from far western Nepal, who are trying their best to sell the Chief and his wife elaborate whisky jugs of burled wood and hammered brass. Soon we're drinking arak and beer together, and language barriers melt into laughter. Suddenly, we're interrupted by a noise that seems to come from the void. It plays in my ears, huge yet light, and the earth matches it by trembling and shaking. Everyone stops.

"Earthquake," says Tanzin, and we look at one another with fear. I've never felt one before, and my mind is thrown back to the devastation that took place in 2015 that caused buildings in this region to collapse like dominos. Luckily, the earth settles herself. Nothing has fallen off the walls, and the roofs are intact. I fall asleep with a clear evacuation plan in the front of my mind. Just in case.

Serang Monastery, September 27

Today, Tanzin and I will follow a farmer up the locals' path toward Serang Monastery. This route will be short but steep, with 1000 metres of elevation gain. Though Tanzin has crossed Larkye Pass on the main trail over 30 times, he's never been up this offshoot valley that will take us close to the Tibet border and to the other side of Sringi Himal/Tashi Palsang/Chamar. The trail is thin and overgrown, and soon my black hiking pants are covered with sharp burrs and furry seeds to the point where they are so textured they look like an ugly Christmas sweater. (Yes, Tanzin's pants still look clean. How does he do it?) We cross the Serang River on an unstable wooden footbridge, then begin the big ascent up one side of the chasm. Partway up, the farmer stops. Here he will build a stone fence to contain his animals.

Tanzin and I continue alone. The path begins to reveal hidden caves, overhangs and dripping waterfalls adorning the mountainside. This zone reminds me of the jungles and cliffs in Thailand I explored in my early 20s. Bulbous stalactites and rock formations animate the landscape, and we find sacred spots marked by prayer flags, katas and exquisite *mani* stones – carved slabs leaned up against long walls to inspire pilgrims and travellers. One is meant to circle them clockwise to gain merit. The mani stones in Serang have expertly carved images of Buddhas, yogis, and Vajradhara, who is a form of the Buddha who symbolizes the most primordial level of the mind. A female consort holds him in sexual embrace as they realize Buddha nature together.

As we gain the ridge, we come to an overhung stone amphitheatre. Rain falls in gossamer droplets from ferns and grasses high above, and there is an altar of mani stones at the base. This place we've found is called the "self-arisen secret cave of Guru Rinpoche." The self-arisen part must refer to a massive phallus-shaped stalactite. There's no mistaking it: it hangs down with impressive length, girth and a distinctive bulbous head. I'm glad we've taken the hard path to get to Serang Monastery, since it is full of sacred symbols. And they aren't only male. A place where water flows off geometric ledges is called the "Miraculous water of the five classes of Dakinis," and there is a cliff area with "Dakini Vajra-Varahi's secret symbol," a beautifully immodest protrusion that looks like folded labia. Other features include a rock that holds the key to the Hidden Valley of Happiness (Kyimolung), a conch shell, and Dakini (Khandro) footprints.

We hear bells in the forest. A very old woman is tending her cows. We don't concern her as she goes about her work, letting her cattle graze on the green feast all around. She hardly notices us and seems unreal, perhaps a khandro herself who protects this place. We come to a place called "108 mani stones," though there appear to be many more than that. Families from Bihi each commission a stone. When someone dies, the remains are cremated, and whatever is left after the fire is ground up, made into a paste, formed into a little shape and then placed amid the gaps between the stones – a longstanding tradition of this region. The stones are bathed in mist, and I walk around them, paying my respects and letting my eyes soak up the images of dancing Buddhas in a place where human form and stone have become one.

The hike seems to go on forever. Tanzin and I begin to wonder if we'll ever get to Serang Monastery. We come to a metal suspension bridge and walk to the middle.

"It's so far down to the water!" I say.

"Look, Jane!" Below us we can see the remains of a wooden bridge clinging to the sides. The middle has completely given way, leaving it connected only on the sides. It looks like it's out of an Indiana Jones movie.

"I'm glad we didn't have to use that bridge," I say, as a spring of fear erupts in me and throbs and pulses through my veins as I view the rotten wood above an imminent death fall into the abyss.

We spot Serang in the distance, a large complex of temple buildings settled into the green at the foot of enormous peaks. We struggle with the feeling that we are cheating when we don't circumambulate all of the numerous mani walls between us and the monastery due to exhaustion. First, we come to school grounds for lay children, and then we arrive at a main gate. It's locked, so we hop the fence. Before us is a large central courtyard. Inside is a beautiful, three-tiered pagoda that looks quite different than most Tibetan Buddhist temples in this region. Imagine three stacked squares, the biggest at the bottom, then getting smaller at the top. It is painted white with black window trims, and the front doors are open, revealing a dark, mystical space inside. Before we can explore the temple, we are invited to a nearby building to be received. Tanzin and I remove our muddy boots at the entrance to a kitchen building, then press our sweaty footprints onto the plank floor. Orange flames lick the iron stove, and we let ourselves receive the warmth. A ruby-cheeked nun with sparkling eyes serves us tea. Kittens scurry about, then suckle their mother, who basks in the stove's warmth. A massively hairy big black dog wanders from person to person, looking for food scraps and attention. It seems that animals are very loved here. Nearby on a grassy slope, wild Himalayan tahr (a goat-antelope-looking animal) mingle with resting mules, and together they nibble at the food provided by the monastery. Here the wild and domestic bridge their differences. The code of nonviolence is alive and well at Serang, and the animals seem pleased.

Even this remote monastery has not escaped construction season. Outside is the cacophony of chainsaws, hammers and sanders. There is also a loud *puja* ceremony (chanting of prayers) being belted out of a loudspeaker. I had imagined from my friend Yeshe's descriptions that Serang would be a peaceful place of solitude, but inside the walls of this place it is anything but. Tanzin and I sit a little awkwardly in the kitchen room eating huge plates of dal bhat. One of the construction workers comes in for dinner with his friend. He's tall and a little intimidating. He sits at the stove and asks the nun to heat some alcohol.

"The nuns don't mind them drinking?" I whisper to Tanzin.

"I don't think so," he replies, and in the end even we try a little. We are told that about 10–15 trekking groups make the side trip up to Serang annually. There are four reincarnate lamas (or tulkus) of Serang, and the main lama, Karma Rinpoche, is currently in solitary retreat nearby.

I'd told Tanzin that I'd like to spend time in meditation once at Serang. But now that we're here, I have the distinct feeling I'd rather leave. Not that it isn't beautiful, but the construction is intense, the noise, overwhelming. Instead of an idyllic Shangri-La-like experience, we've come to a work zone. The entire courtyard is littered with stones, and the work pace is almost feverish. In itself, all this work is actually a sign of a healthy, thriving community. But the wildness of Sarphu is still potent in my mind. I'm most at home where there are no buildings at all. Where nature and its contact with one's mind becomes the main teacher.

At bedtime, I'm given a giant Thermos of hot water, and then I retreat to a guest room. Himalayan people seem to revere the Thermos. They have many inside their homes. They spend much time boiling water and filling multiple Thermoses so they can have a near steady stream of butter tea all day long. The Thermoses are amazingly well made and keep water at a near boiling temperature for a long time. Mine is plugged with a plastic-wrapped cork. The cork is caked with layers of soot and grime, but I'm thrilled to have autonomy over my own hot water.

Before sleep, I creep into the darkness to find the bathroom. It seems no one has been to the guest toilets in recent history. There are three doors. One says VIP, so naturally I try that one first. No luck; the door is locked. The middle one has an open padlock that I remove. Inside, a shower head protrudes from the wall. There's a pedestal sink and a Western-style toilet. All are in disrepair. I turn on the tap and water shoots out the pipe and sprays my pants. I wash the toilet seat with some precious toilet paper before I dare sit (I swear, there's a benefit to squat toilets!), and after spending a few minutes in that room, and smelling its attendant odours, I decide a shower isn't so necessary after all.

Meeting the Protectors, September 28

We are insulated and held at bay by more wet weather. A brass monastery gong vibrates through the mist. I head to the temple to immerse myself in Serang's activities. I walk through the doors and enter a lake of maroon robes. The nuns sit on the left, the monks, on the right. At the centre of the room is a huge mandala (three-dimensional representation of the mind and the universe), and it reminds me of how Kyimolung beyul can be viewed as a mandala with coinciding layers of awareness. A painter's brush has decorated the temple walls with images of the Mahasiddhas – historical wild yogis and yoginis who were brave enough to break rules, tradition and societal roles to find the true nature of their minds. I love these hippie-like characters, with their topknots and illicit behaviours. They were rebels, not conformists. I look up to the ceiling and see a sun on the right side and moon on the left, corresponding to the male and female symbols in both Tibetan Buddhism and the Himalayan Indian yoga tradition I teach.

I'm offered a seat next to the novice nuns and some kids. There's no cushion for me to sit on, so an old nun shoves me almost onto the lap of a young child so we can share a pillow. The child looks horrified, and as soon as the nun leaves I ease my way back to my own personal bubble of space. The ritual begins. I feel quite nervous being the only outsider and not knowing what this particular ritual represents. At times, we are handed grains that we throw into the air in a grain shower. I throw a little too vigorously, and the grain hits a nun in the row in front of me. I feel a bit naughty and a bit confined. My hips ache, then release. Ache, then release. After the ritual, Tanzin and I are taken up a hill to a beautiful house. It is here that two young reincarnate lamas live. I feel almost like I'm in a beachside Malaysian villa when I see the shiny tile veranda of their private residence. It's immaculately clean and in stark contrast to the remote wilderness of this mountain environment. Here we meet the young monks. One is the reincarnation of the former head and spiritual master of Serang Monastery, Chokyi Nyima Rinpoche. I'm so surprised – they are barely teenagers. Their left eyes have bandages on them, and when Tanzin asks about this, they look shy and a bit embarrassed. We are told that it's meant to protect their eyesight, since they are doing so much studying. We offer katas and little money envelopes as is customary. One of them puts the scarf back over my neck and touches my temples as a blessing.

We take the rest of the day to interview monastics and explore. When Tanzin and I had asked people in Tsum about Tashi Palsang, only a few people seemed to know the mountain by this name. It was more commonly called by the Nepali name, Sringi Himal. But everyone here calls it Tashi Palsang, and it is hugely revered.

We sit with an old lama named Pema Gyamtso, who has lived at Serang for 27 years. He tells us he was once married, but his wife died when he was 33 years old, so he became a monk. He confirms that Sarphu is the main place where Kyimolung's treasures have been revealed, and that the maximum treasures are held within Tashi Palsang. Since Serang Monastery is located at the foot of Tashi Palsang on its western side, it is considered a sacred location, and the monastics feed the land and its spirits prayers and ritual offerings, and protect it with their lives and their presence.

"All this land, from Manaslu to Kyirong in Tibet, is Guru Rinpoche's [Padmasambhava's] land," says Pema. We chat with him until the gong calls him back for yet another ritual. The monastic schedule is rigorous, with only a few short breaks between prayers.

I leave the fireside and walk up a set of steps to a little temple building. I open the doors and am greeted by a golden statue of Padmasambhava. Light cascades down to his crown and shoulders from high windows; a table of glimmering butter lamps casts a honey glow. They flicker now and then from the wind that creeps through the cracks of the doors. The wall panels are painted with Buddhas and yogis, and I sit down to join them.

The unstoppable rain has halted construction today, and there is relative quiet. I settle into this place and into my body as I sit cross-legged on the ground. I'm back at Tashi Palsang. The mountain has a steady power I can feel when I am quiet. I drop into meditation and begin to feel that I am breathing the mountain into my heart, then out of my heart, as if the regular boundaries of stone and flesh have melted. My veins become glacial rivers. My heart is full of treasure.

After a while, I get the distinct feeling I'm being watched. I open my eyes to see five round, little faces pressing against the glass. I leave my meditation and go outside to play. The children who have been watching me pull up their shirts and stick out their bellies to show me an impressive array of chicken pox. I try to distract them from their scratching by showing them photos of Alberta's Rocky Mountains and videos of my kids skiing.

A monk offers to take Tanzin and me for a tour of the main temple. The ground floor represents the nirmanakaya realm, which is the physical realm humans see and relate to in this world. This is where I had sat during the morning ritual. At the back of the room is a wooden ladder. We ascend. On the second level there is a statue of the Buddha of Compassion (Chenrezig). This layer represents the sambhogakaya realm, the "enjoyment" realm of the Buddhas. We walk to the outside balcony and circumambulate the temple. Then we climb to the third and highest level. This symbolizes the dharmakaya realm – the realm of total enlightenment. Up here sits a golden statue of Samantabhadra intertwined with a beautiful blue consort. The lama who is in retreat, Karma Rinpoche, later tells me (after I'm back in Canada) that this Buddha and consort are like the symbolic parents of all the many Buddhas in the Tibetan Buddhist pantheon. By knowing their nature, one knows the nature of all things and achieves enlightenment. Their bodies are smooth and at ease in their embrace, and they hold themselves together in perpetual bliss. The statue seems to hum at the base of my eardrums, emitting a state of rapture. It's a suggestion of the vividness we could all experience if we had the courage to drop the veils within our own minds. We circumambulate the tiny upper chamber.

All day long the gong has dissected time into calls-to-practice, its brass voice pulling monastics into the temple like a maroon tide. There is laughter and a sense of joy that beams from their cheeks, which have been tinted pink by high altitude. Their devotion isn't heavy. Their lives are synched to the rituals they believe will protect the holy mountain behind their temple. They have promised their time on this earth to guarding Padmasambhava's treasures and living out their teachings. Multiple retreat huts surround this place, and both female and male practitioners can dissolve from the world for a time to explore the inner workings of their minds.

The ethic here is peace, diligence and a clear tenderness for the abundant animals. But make no mistake: they are not naive pushovers drifting in hippie bliss. They protect the mountain with practice and, if needed, force. Let's recall the past attempts to summit Tashi Palsang. The only successful attempt was in 1954 (again, not recognized by the Nepal government), and those climbers approached from the east as Tanzin and I had. In 2000, a group of climbers got a permit from the Nepali government to climb Tashi Palsang from this western approach I am now on. But the Serang lamas forbid them.

Despite having a valid permit from the Nepalese Ministry of Tourism & Civil Aviation to climb the West Face of Chamar, 7187 m, on arrival in the Sringi Khola [river], where they planned to establish a base camp, the local Lama would not allow this team to attempt it. Learning that if they continued they might be stoned to death, discretion deemed it advisable to try approaching the mountain from a different side. Unfortunately, the [east] side turned out to be in the same high-avalanche-risk condition reported by a British expedition six years earlier...As a result the attempt was aborted at 5900 m.[38]

I think about the lamas in this *Alpine Journal* report who bravely said, NO! You cannot come to our holy place for the purpose of climbing. I watch as they continue to serve as protectors 19 years later and, hopefully, far, far into the future.

Tanzin and I walk to the kitchen and settle ourselves in while monks and nuns deposit stories with us. My purpose here is not to conquer and rename a mountain. It is to soak up their stories and way of life. Rather than leaving marks of Jane here, I want Kyimolung to leave its marks on me.

We share our own hard-earned stories of Sarphu with these people on this other side of the mountain. The extreme geographic barriers between this side of Tashi Palsang and the other side mean that different stories have been preserved, and Tanzin doesn't even recognize some of the words here in Nubri, since the language evolved slightly differently from the Tsum side.

"On one side, they don't know much about the other side," Tanzin remarks. "It's so good that you are getting so much reliable information from both."

Back to the Main Trail, September 29

We wake at Serang, then leave the monks and nuns as they supplicate Kyimolung and descend for 24 kilometres to meet the pulsing

---

38 Bill Ruthven, "Mount Everest Foundation Expedition Reports 2000," *The Alpine Journal*, 2020, 285–295, https://www.alpinejournal.org. uk/Contents/Contents_2001_files/AJ%202001%20285-295%20 MEF%20Reports.pdf.

waters of the Budhi Gandaki. Then over the next days we follow the well-worn route toward Mount Manaslu. I notice our gear is looking pretty abused. Tanzin's new Scarpa shoes are splitting at the seams. Down leaks from our jackets, puffy little feathers finding their way out of little tears and holes. Everything is smoke-soaked from Sarphu, and the original colour of our gear is now hidden beneath layers of brown and grey. Hundreds of sticky burrs have worked their way into the fibres of my two pairs of pants. My gear is so far from its glossy and expensive berth on the store shelves of Canada. It has lost its shine, but it has gained character.

Lho Village, October 1

I wake to views of mighty Mount Manaslu. The clouds shift and reveal the massif slowly, slowly, as I gaze up from my balcony. First, I see the mountain's girth, then, finally, the famous notch between its uppermost peaks. "You are lucky!" says Tanzin. "Many people don't get to see the peak." I feel this whole trip we've been lucky and supported. Everything has happened just so and with little fuss. The more I trust myself, the more things open up all around us.

The trail leads us to the busy village of Samagaun that serves as a base for climbing attempts on Manaslu. A backlog of climbers who are finished their expeditions is waiting for the cloud to clear so they can be helicoptered down to Kathmandu. Tanzin and I eat lunch at a trekking lodge brimming with primary-coloured, North Face dry bags and sunburned climbers eager to return home. I feel tiny and alone among these lanky giants as they log entries and fiddle with satellite phones. I have not achieved something as concrete as they have. My journey silently throbs inside me, and I don't yet know how to talk about it.

We press onward to Samdo village, and the world becomes quiet and spacious again. A seam in the clouds splits, and yellow sun spills down. For the first time, it begins to feel like autumn. We find ourselves in a Canada-like scene of golden-leafed poplars, larches and glinting streams.

We arrive in the high-altitude world of Samdo, at 4460 metres. The landscape is similar to Tibet now, arid and treeless, swept bare by the wind. The Tibet border is only a day's walk from here. I love how the hem-like border of Tibet keeps pulling us up chasmic valleys like a magnet. There must be something in my bones that's high Himalayan or Tibetan, for when the trekking trail drops us low, to where it's warm and humid, my body becomes tired, my spirits low. Strangely, it's when the trees give way and the stone becomes dominant, when the views become dangerous and wild, that's when my heart really sings.

The trekking accommodations in Samdo are set like a false front before the traditional village. They are mostly a ramshackle mess of poorly built structures, and little thought has been given to organization or function. A set of rooms here, an adjoining hallway there, as if the builder were only planning one room at a time. We find a concrete building under construction. It's too new to have any character, and is made of solid concrete, like a bunker. But it's clean and offers views toward Larkye Bazaar, an old marketplace used for trade between Tibet and Nepal. There is a frontier feeling here.

The next day, we're invited into the Nepali kitchen and offered tea. There's an adorable, chubby baby, and soon I'm bouncing her on my knee. She offers up big, open smiles. A Nepali traveller pops his head in the kitchen and smiles at us, asking, "Your baby?" In the kitchen, huddled with the workers around a gigantic metal stove, we meet yet another local leader named Nyima Dorjee (the baby's father). The ward Chiefs and village leaders Tanzin keeps introducing me to have been salt-of-the-earth people trying to navigate new village autonomy and some of the power granted by the newly democratic Nepal government. Nyima is no exception. He's well educated and well spoken. His hair is cropped short, and he, too, has a good collection of keys strung on his belt. We tell him about our journey to Sarphu (news hasn't spread this far) and learn that Nyima is well versed on Kyimolung and very interested in our tales. We ask for what name he calls Tashi Palsang, and he says, "Sringi," giving us a new explanation behind the meaning of the name of the holy treasure mountain.

"Sring, refers to Serang, and ki (gi) means belonging to," he says. "So Sringi is the mountain belonging to Serang." This is yet a different definition, and I think of the rigorous rituals at Serang Monastery and their undying protection of the mountain.

Nyima tells us about the old Kyimolung pilgrimage route that crosses the border near here, goes into and then east through Tibet, comes out in upper Tsum, travels down the main Tsum Valley, and finally connects with what is now the Manaslu trekking route.[39] "The older people of Samdo want to make this pilgrimage, so I am helping them. We want to be allowed to travel the Kyimolung pilgrimage route through Tibet. Last year, we had a border conference with Tibetan officials, and the result was very positive. We think this will be possible by 2020."

The Chinese government restricts border access into Tibet, and it has been years since the entire route has been accessible to Nepali Himalayans. Now Nyima is taking on the challenge of getting special permission for his people to walk the outer petals of the lotus flower of Kyimolung in a great clockwise circumambulation.

The officials he's dealing with come from the district of Kyirong, Tibet, just east of Tsum – where my own teacher's monastery is located. It is a long and beautiful valley next to Tsum, and many of Padmasambhava's treasures have been revealed there. Kyirong lies just outside Kyimolung's boundaries, and it did not enjoy the protection that Tsum and Nubri had during the horrors of the Cultural Revolution and Chinese takeover of Tibet. Its monasteries were destroyed. Practitioners were arrested or killed. I'm grateful to hear that time seems to be releasing old traumas in that area, and that spiritual bonds are (hopefully) being renewed.

---

39 The Kyimolung pilgrimage route is different than accessing Tashi Palsang and the core of the beyul. It travels around the mountain in a massive circumambulation.

"I am going to personally check this route and make a map," says Nyima. "I must count the rivers and check safety. I will be wilderness camping because there are no facilities in that part of Tibet. I'm worried about how hard it will be for the older people, but I will try my best." Nyima was supposed to meet with the Kyirong officials this very day, but the meeting has been delayed until tomorrow. He's optimistic that he'll get their final seal of approval. Kyimolung beyul seems to be opening herself to those who long to go inside. Nyima's wire-rimmed glasses glint as he contemplates his task. "It's my karmic and dharmic work. My biggest wish. To reconnect the pilgrimage route." What was once sliced off by the Chinese Communist colonization of Tibet may soon be stitched back together.

Nyima is currently serving as the caretaker of the local Samdo Monastery, named Tega Pema Choeling,[40] and he agrees to take us there. We walk through the stone village on the edge of a valley that leads to Samdo Peak (5177 metres). Tanzin comments that the architecture here is unique. "The windows are so small to keep in the warmth. It looks like a combination of Tibetan and Nepali styles."

The temple sits in a spot of honour, highest among the village buildings. Its stone walls are smudged white, and the door is painted in cheerful reds and blues. Nyima unlocks the door. I unlace my hiking boots, and even though Nyima says I need not worry, I take my shoes off anyway as an act of reverence. Blood contracts from my feet when they touch the cold planks.

The main altar is home to numerous extremely old, rare and beautiful statues. I'm drawn to a creamy-coloured statue of Milarepa. He sits with his hand to his ear, listening, and his expression is relaxed yet anticipatory.

The original inhabitants of Samdo come from a village just over the Tibet border called Rue. During the Cultural Revolution in

---

40 It was originally the Kagyu branch of Tibetan Buddhism, but is now a combination of the Kagyu and Nyingma branches, called Kanying.

Tibet, their monastery was destroyed. "Tega Monastery in Tibet was a very big institution. More than 1,000 years old," Nyima tells us. He estimates that the invading Chinese army destroyed two-thirds of the monastery's texts and statues. The Rue people gathered what they could, then fled across the border and survived by living in caves. Even before they built themselves permanent shelter, they put their efforts into building this temple to save the surviving texts. Thus, in the 1960s, this temple was constructed.

"At that time, the people didn't have materials or skills. They didn't have masons, carpenters, and I don't even know how they did it. Look at the paintings. They've done very well," he says with obvious pride. "It was totally difficult!"

An entire wall is adorned with cubbyholes that house Buddhist texts. Nyima shows us the elaborately carved covers that hold loose pages of scripture together.

"The texts are terma. They were pulled from caves behind Tega Monastery in Tibet. Chinese soldiers burned many of the texts and scattered them across the ground, exposing them to the elements. They got wet, stepped on – it was a very evil deed. My personal view is that the texts are most important. If there are no statues in the world, that doesn't matter. But we cannot memorize all the teachings that show the path to Nirvana."[41] Some of the wooden book covers that were thrown about the earth fell into a river, then floated from Tibet to Nepal, as if wanting to be reunited with their caretakers. The exiled villagers collected them, resorted thousands of pieces of paper into their original order, then placed them into the wall before us. Tanzin and I have been wandering the mountains and treasure locations, and now we are actually seeing Padmasambhava's revealed treasures. I get shivers as I look at the volumes in the wall. I walk to them and bow down, my forehead making contact with an immense history.

---

41 Nyima says the tertön was likely Chokyi Lingpa, but the Samdo villagers have not yet found a written history confirming the tertön, or the story of how the treasure texts were revealed.

As we leave the village, Nyima points up valley toward Samdo peak. "There is a climbing team back there now. Local people believe there are protector deities in the mountains, and that they are unhappy with the climbers. That is why the weather is bad this year." Nyima tells me he puts pressure on the Kathmandu-based climbing companies to dispose of their oxygen canisters and garbage, and tells them that if he finds garbage up there, he will tell the government, and they won't get any more permits. Like the deities, he's a fierce protector too.

Before we say our goodbyes, Nyima tells us about a rock we will see after Larkye Pass. He calls it the Western Gate Protector. Until now, I have not been able to pinpoint the Western Gate of Kyimolung beyul.

"There is a big rock above some black cliffs," explains Nyima. "It looks like a man wearing a Tibetan hat and guards the Western Gate. We place stones there in offering. Watch for it." We make a mental note, say our goodbyes, then ascend to Dharamshala, the last outpost before Larkye Pass.

Dharamshala is a tiny little place pocked with vinyl-sided industrial shacks. I open the door to my room to find a mattress set upon a bed of stones. It looks freezing cold, but I open up my sleeping bag, crawl in and feel surprisingly comfortable. Mike and I satellite message each other, and he jokes that I'll be just fine, since I like sleeping in rocky places.

There are other trekkers here, all waiting in anticipation of the big climax of the Manaslu trek that will come tomorrow. We huddle around long tables, wearing layers of down and big woollen hats. The consensus is that most groups will wake just before 4 a.m. to begin their ascent.

Tanzin leans over to me and says, "We'll have breakfast at 8 or 9. You are very fast." I feel a little pride. Unfortunately, the kitchen staff don't want to have two breakfast shifts – one for the other trekkers and one for Tanzin and me. After their early morning cooking session, they would rather go back to sleep.

Larkye Pass, October 3

At 4:30 a.m. I crack open my door and see stars flickering in the black sky. Thank god, it has stopped raining. I hope for crystal views of these great mountains before I leave Kyimolung. My breath freezes in the subzero temperatures. The other trekkers depart, while Tanzin and I fuel up on food and two cups of instant coffee, then head into a world that for now is only the size of the beam stretching from our lamps.

The sun begins to lighten the immense peaks all around us, and the world expands. I pant in the thin air, wispy, white-blue breaths and a jumping heart. I feel a surge inside that is strangely competitive. Perhaps it was Tanzin's comments about my speed. Or perhaps it's because I'm ready to get down now, to write about Kyimolung, to incorporate all I've learned and to see my family. I feel like a runner at the end of a race. I want to get to Larke Pass first. We blast past all the trekkers who had set out before us. I'm relentless. My legs become pumps, strong from every step I took in Tsum and Serang. I'm strong from years of study, prostration practice, gruelling Himalayan treks of purification, mistakes, more study, desolate longing for these mountains and never knowing if or when I would return, vomiting and diarrhea, wet tents, flea bites, smelly feet, missing my children, missing Mike. My lungs are efficient, my blood acclimatized. I feel unapologetically strong, and it feels fucking great. I'm at the crux, and I'm facing it head on.

We follow a frozen trail through a world of glaciers and rock, a world so still that little lakes become perfect mirrors of the world around them. I see myself in them too – all the beautiful and all the ugly.

And then I see it. A line of potently coloured prayer flags and a sign reading, "Larkye Pass (5106 m). Welcome to Manaslu Conservation Area, wish you happy journey." When we reach it, I realize the pass is less steep and demanding than I'd imagined.

Having reached the pass, we linger. The other groups filter up, take photos and then overtake us, but now I'm at ease. Something is settling inside me. We make a slow descent, and I swirl through the high-altitude moonscape, taking time to soak up all I see. We reach the black cliffs Nyima had told us about, and meet the Western Gate Protector. He looms tall from his spot above the trail, and his Tibetan hat forms a line in the sky. He is saying goodbye. My time in the beyul has come to an end. I pull a kata from my pack, but it catches in the zipper, as if hesitant to be released. I finally extract the errant white strands from the zipper teeth, then I climb a boulder and reach, stretching my arms to the highest part of a trail marker. I tie the scarf there as a gesture of thanks, and as my final offering. We have been so supported throughout our journey. As we relaxed into Kyimolung's earthy, challenging environment, it opened for us – and within us too. The kata undulates in the wind. Feelings of gratitude flow like nectar through every part of me.

We walk down a long moraine, past three great arms of the Ponkar Glacier to the confluence where they merge into one. When viewed aerially, these glaciers look like Guru Rinpoche's trident. The river has merged back into one.

Letting Go, October 4

I sleep long and hard in a pretty guest house that has a balcony wound through with nasturtiums. This will be our last day of trekking. We descend and enter the Annapurna Sanctuary, and suddenly I find myself walking through a fairyland of fluted, white peaks backed by strong blue sky. Streams rush past, tinkling in the sunlight. I hike ahead and alone for a long time, deep into the forest.

"Today is the last day in the mountains," Tanzin had said in the morning, and now he's giving me space, walking somewhere far behind me. A great processing begins as I walk solo. It starts in the form of tears. There is a tangible pull as I feel my body getting further and further from the great Himalayan ranges. Sometimes

I sing, sometimes a sob squeaks out. And, finally, after hours of this emotional dance, the mountains release me.

We descend 28 kilometres from Bimthang to Dharapani and collapse at a guest house. The next day, we take a gruelling Jeep ride on a road not really fit for a vehicle. I've travelled roads like this before, and I feel a familiar fear, a tightness in my body. Tanzin has advised me to sit on the mountainside back seat, while he bobs up and down in the passenger seat – cliffside.

"Are you scared?" I ask him.

"No, not scary," he replies. I'm more terrified now than I was upon any of Sarphu's ridges. I trusted my own hands there, in the wilderness, but now my life is in the hands of a very young driver who says he must drink lots of arak at bedtime to ease the pain in his body (from bouncing and grinding along this road) to be able to fall asleep. Occupational hazard.

We survive the road and arrive at the lakeside town of Pokhara. I have transformed from avid, high-altitude trekker to swamp monster. It is steaming hot here compared to the mountains. I'm more sweat, mud and dung than I am Jane. My hiking boots, having served me so very well on the trail, now feel clunky and oppressive, and my clothes are so completely dirty that I worry the bohemian travellers in their pretty blouses and hemp shirts will run screaming. I find a corner shop where I buy shampoo, face wash, deodorant and a razor. The cashier looks at me knowingly as I fork over some rupees. At night, I leave my sleeping bag in its stuff sack and tuck myself under a white duvet. A final monsoon rain unleashes, and I fall asleep to the sound of so much water and dream of my friend Drakar Rinpoche. I wonder and hope about seeing him back in Kathmandu.

Kathmandu, October 9

I awake with a sense of trust on my final day in Nepal. Last night, Tanzin and I went to the Hindu cremation grounds at Pashupati Temple, where we attended a ritual and watched bodies burning in the firelight. The scene was strangely comforting: the bodies settled on platforms in the open air; the lighting of the pyre by a family member; the remnants of hair and bone in the flames; the smoke and ash floating past the temple spires and then to the open sky. This pivotal transformation of solid body to ash in just one hour was much faster than I'd thought. Just think: in one hour, your entire physical body can be returned to its elements. This knowledge gives me mental freedom. Today, I trust those natural forces of birth, life, death, and the love that transcends them. I long to see Drakar Rinpoche before I leave Nepal on the night plane. I am tender as the final release begins.

After breakfast, Tanzin picks me up on his motorbike. I sit behind him, and he tells me I can hold his backpack straps. His body is a strong mountain body, and his driving is confident and steady. This time he asks me, "Are you scared?" And I reply with honesty, "No, not scary." We enter the hive of Kathmandu, sliding in beside taxis and other motorcycles, dodging latent cows and darting dogs, and maneuvering between cracks in the concrete and bumps in the dirt roads. I feel so alive on the back of Tanzin's bike.

We await Rinpoche at the Monkey Temple, a famous stupa in Swayambhunath, close to where he lives. I explain to Tanzin that Rinpoche is not like other lamas; he is shy, a little unreliable and is not a monk. Rinpoche lives simply, and has almost nothing to his name. He cannot inhabit his rightful monastery just over the Tsum border in Tibet due to ongoing political issues. Recently, he's even had to move out of his apartment due to a rent increase.

"He's here," says Tanzin, spotting him first. Inside the cavity of my chest, my heart stutters and does a somersault. Rinpoche has his long hair pulled into a low ponytail. He's wearing jeans, a maroon jacket, a hat and a smile. We offer him katas. He places Tanzin's around Tanzin's neck, and tucks mine away to keep. We must follow him to his new apartment. "I will bike. You ride with Tanzin and follow me," he says. He hops on his bicycle and begins pedalling down a hill. I can't help but break into a massive grin. He's biking so fast! Rinpoche is very tall and has long legs, and his pace is amazing. He leads us down curling alleyways to his home and invites us in. Rinpoche has made us a lunch of *momos* (Tibetan dumplings), and in a major role reversal for Tibetan Buddhism, *he* serves *us*. I am touched by how Rinpoche chooses to exist in this world – his humble nature, his kind eyes.

We chat and catch up on news, and Tanzin gives Rinpoche information on obtaining a local border card that allows Tsumpas to cross into Tibet. The walking distance from Tsum to Rinpoche's monastery in Tibet is one day, yet he hasn't been there in many years. The last time he tried, he was arrested, held and told that, if he ever came back, he must obtain special permission. As they chat in Tibetan, I pray that Rinpoche will get to make a trip to his monastery one day soon.

I have a hope inside, a wish for this meeting. I've been waiting a long time to receive a Tibetan name. When I met Ken in Naapi's land in southern Alberta, he told me about the name the Piikani had given him: Buffalo Runner. Such a loving connection he'd made with the Indigenous People of that region. I told Ken that I longed to be given a name. Perhaps the need for a name came from my need for land, for the ancestry I search for. "It will come at the right time," he'd said with confidence.

Finally, that time has come for me.

Rinpoche looks at me. He's been thinking about it a long time too. "Sonam Chödon," he says. "Sonam means lucky, and chö means dharma. Don means light, like a small butter lamp that lights the way for others." And so I receive my name – *lucky one whose light shines the way for others*. There is so much goodness in this name. I've been lucky to have made it to the core of Kyimolung beyul. I have followed Guru Rinpoche's instructions and found the sacred locations. Ani Pema's last name is Chödron, so now my sister and I share the same last name. The nunnery where she lives is called Drephuet Dronme, the *dron* or *don* specifically referring to the fact her nunnery was the very first built in Tsum, and it ignited the Buddhist teachings that are said to light the way for people who seek enlightenment.

"You like it?" asks Rinpoche.

"I love it," I reply.

He gives me a burgundy scarf and a medallion from Bhutan. We share a hug, and his body feels so skinny in our embrace. The feeling I have for Rinpoche is big and old, and goes back before time.

We walk to the main street together, and I hop on the motorcycle as Jane Sonam Chödon. I reach out for Rinpoche one last time. He takes my hand, wraps it up warmly and gives it a squeeze. Then I hold onto Tanzin as we speed into the throng.

EPILOGUE

Nature has touched me so deeply that she won't let me return to what was. How can one leave Shangri-La? Like my grandpa, I have pined for a place in nature. A settling into my own Happy Valley and, thus, into my own skin.

My husband and I ask big, scary questions. What do we want for our children, who are now teenagers? How do we want them to experience this world? What's truly important for us? Over the winter, our family makes many trips to the Rocky Mountains to fly over untouched powder fields on our backcountry skis, and to race down double black diamonds at Sunshine Village in Banff. We watch our children light up in the mountains. We watch them thrive. So our little group of four makes a big decision. With our eyes turned southwest, we decide to relocate to the mountain town of Canmore. We will be cradled in the Bow Valley amid ancient geology and an Indigenous history reaching back more than 10,000 years. When we creep down nearby canyons, we'll be able to see pictographs and to wash our faces in the outflow of glaciers. I ask the Bow Valley to take us in. I ask it to become our Happy Valley.

I make several trips from our new home to Head-Smashed-In Buffalo Jump/Pisskà'n to meet with Conrad Little Leaf, learning the original place names of Naapi's land and incorporating them into my book. On the final vetting of the Alberta section, he bestows upon me a Soki-tapi name, Iitsspahpowaawahkaa – Walking Above. I've been given not one new name, but two, and they strike at the core of who I am. They embody me, and that embodiment connects me to the land and the ones who know it with such astounding intimacy. My names weave me into a great story, and I hope this story weaves into you, so we can all become kin, a family of protectors and lovers of the earth.

For all the wild ones who long for Shangri-La, my wish is this: May we discover our own happy valleys, and when we do, may we touch them with love, so they can remain happy for generations to come. May they stay pristine so others can return to nature in times of need. And may all who search for Shangri-La find it, whether it's located in a physical space, or within the depths of the heart.

GLOSSARY AND LINKS

beyul: Paradisiacal hidden valleys consecrated in the eighth century by the Buddhist yogi Padmasambhava, also called Guru Rinpoche.

chöd: A tantric Buddhist practice that means slaying or cutting off. Refers to the ego. Traditionally, chöd practitioners go to frightening places, such as a cemetery, and they visualize making their body into an offering.

gompa: House of meditation; a temple.

lama: A Buddhist teacher.

neyig/neyik: A place guide describing Padmasambhava's beyuls.

rinpoche: A reincarnate lama or high teacher.

stupa/chorten: A layered Buddhist structure sometimes containing relics.

terma: Teachings hidden by Guru Rinpoche and his consort Yeshe Tsogyal that are important in Tibetan Buddhism.

tertön: Treasure finders who often have dreams about the location of terma and the ability to reveal the hidden treasure.

The Compassion Project

Started in 2015, this Canadian registered charity is run by Jane and a small group of Tsumpas, with the aim of improving health care and education.

WEBSITE: compassionfortsum.ca
EMAIL: compassionfortsum@gmail.com
INSTAGRAM: thecompassionproject_tsum_
FACEBOOK: @compassionfortsum

Jane Marshall

WEBSITE: seejanewrite.ca
INSTAGRAM: @janeandthemountains
FACEBOOK: facebook.com/see.write

Karuna Mountain Adventures

Jane started a family business after writing this book to give people the chance to visit Tsum and other special locations. Join Tanzin for your own great adventure!

WEBSITE: seejanewrite.ca/karunamountainadventures
INSTAGRAM: @karunamountainadventures
EMAIL: karunamountainadventures@gmail.com

Amouddou Trekking, Morocco

Ahmad El-Allaly, guide (English and French)
WEBSITE: amouddou-trekking.com
EMAIL: amouddou.trekking@gmail.com

SELECTED SOURCES

Baker, I. *The Heart of the World: A Journey to Tibet's Lost Paradise.* New York: Penguin, 2004.

Bastien, B. *Blackfoot Ways of Knowing: The Worldview of the Siksikaitsitapi.* Calgary: University of Calgary Press, 2004.

Blaxley, B. *The Whaleback: A Walking Guide.* Victoria: Rocky Mountain Books, 1997.

Daschuk, J. *Clearing the Plains: Disease, Politics of Starvation, and the Loss of Indigenous Life.* Regina: University of Regina Press, 2013.

McLuhan, T.C. *The Way of the Earth: Encounters with Nature in Ancient and Contemporary Thought.* New York: Simon and Schuster, 1994.

Rosen, K. *With You By Bike.* Victoria: Rocky Mountain Books, 2019.

Ross, R. *Indigenous Healing: Exploring Traditional Paths.* Toronto: Penguin, 2014.

Scobie, C. *Last Seen in Lhasa: The Story of an Extraordinary Friendship in Modern Tibet.* London: Rider, 2006.

Strayed, C. *Wild: From Lost to Found on the Pacific Crest Trail.* New York: Vintage Books, 2013.

Zangpo, N. *Guru Rinpoche: His Life and Times.* Ithaca, NY: Snow Lion Publications, 2002.

ABOUT THE AUTHOR

 Jane Marshall has written for the *Edmonton Journal, Travel Alberta, VUE Weekly, Avenue Magazine* and the University of Alberta's *illuminate* magazine, and was the content editor for the *Edmonton Journal* and *Calgary Herald*'s "Capital Ideas" sections. She currently writes an adventure blog for *Breathe Outdoors* to inspire people to connect with nature. Her first book, *Back Over the Mountains* (Hay House India, 2015), introduced her to the Himalayas, and she's been learning about sacred lands ever since. Marshall fell in love with the land and people of Tsum, Nepal, and co-founded the Compassion Project, a Canadian registered charity striving to improve health care and education. Her trekking company, Karuna Mountain Adventures, connects people to the land and people of Nepal so they, too, can experience the Himalayas. She lives in Canmore with her husband and two children, and teaches English to refugees and newcomers. You can find her in the alpine random camping or skiing, or at seejanewrite.ca.